RECOMMENDATIONS:

"In the aftermath of World War Two, missions were easily established on the Bornean coast, but it took some very special people to go into the wild interior with their little children, learn the local languages, and preach and live out the gospel as they translated the precious scriptures, so that this new limb of the body of Christ might become powerful. In remote communities, miracles often took place and this book shines with the exciting light of these amazing times."

Peter Cooper,
Curator of BEM archives and son of the BEM pilot, Ken Cooper

"What a joy to be let into the journey of Jim as he goes back to his parents' missionary roots to see for himself the legacy of planting the gospel in the soil prepared by the Lord. It is producing a crop, 'some thirty, some sixty, and some a hundred times what was sown'. A great encouragement!'"

Reverend Garry Dibley,
Missions Operations Director, CMS NSW & ACT

"The writer is the son of one of the first Australian missionaries who came to Ranau after World War Two to expand the Gospel of God. I definitely recommend Gospel Blaze in Borneo. Each Christian household, especially from the Ranau region, should have a copy."

Paul Kerangkas,
Son of Kerangkas, renowned, indigenous evangelist, and pastor

Gospel Blaze in Borneo

Jim Ward

Ark House Press
arkhousepress.com

Gospel Blaze in Borneo © 2024 Jim Ward

Unless otherwise stated, all Scriptures are taken from the New International Translation (Holy Bible. Copyright© 1996, 2004, 2007, 2013 by Tyndale House Foundation. Used by permission of Tyndale House Publishers Inc., Carol Stream, Illinois 60188. All rights reserved.)

Some names and identifying details have been changed to protect the privacy of individuals.

Cataloguing in Publication Data:
Title: Gospel Blaze in Borneo
ISBN: 9781763620124 (pbk)
Subjects: REL012170 (RELIGION / Christian Living / Personal Memoirs); REL045000 (RELIGION / Christian Ministry / Missions);

Design by initiateagency.com

Illustrations on the front cover sum up the setting for *Gospel Blaze in Borneo*. They show:

Top is BEM pilot Ken Cooper with talented native mechanic Tebari Ukab, standing with an Auster Autocar outside the hangar at mission HQ, Lawas, in Sarawak. Tebari was a genius working with engines and although he had no formal qualifications, he went away to the coast to work under Shell engineers for a while and they were very happy to certify him as aircraft mechanic. A very quiet, hard working man, he spoke and wrote English very well and his reading was excellent. It seems that he never married and he died young from diabetes, from which many Borneans suffered in the days before refrigeration was widespread. Ian Stacey was the relieving pilot seconded to BEM from MAF in PNG for 1963, and he said of Tebari: "I greatly valued his friendship and assistance." Tebari also gave evangelistic and Christian training talks for which he prepared most carefully.

It is fitting that he stands here on equal terms with his pilot brother in Christ, Ken. He was the right man in the right place at just the right time, which sums up the BEM story. The safety of the whole BEM Aviation program that ran for three decades at high intensity in flimsy, fabric covered aircraft without a major incident, is testimony to expert, willing workers to the harvest like Tebari and dedicated, skilful pilots such as Bruce Morton and Ken Cooper.

Below them Sabin holding Ludin smile in safety soon after a vital but quite dangerous first contact outreach along the wild lower Labuk River regions of Sabah in 1955. Ludin was nearly lost to measles fever there, but was wonderfully saved.

Bottom is a tranquil pastoral scene at Ranau, Sabah 1960, which had then become the centre of Gospel Outreach in Sabah that continues to blaze for Jesus today. Fifteen years before this, the rural peace of Ranau was shattered by the Japanese who turned it into the infamous killing fields at the end of the Sandakan death marches, in which many Australians lost their lives.

GOSPEL BLAZE IN BORNEO -
A pilgrim returns to an old mission field,
by Jim Ward, called Ludin,
eldest son of James and Laura Ward,
called Sabin and Kumin, who were
pioneer missionaries in the early 1950s
to the interior of Sabah, East Malaysia,
for the Borneo Evangelical Mission.

For all the Mission Kids who, without choice, had to accept the sufferings and cultural shocks resulting from the vision, commitment, sacrifices and also the very human mistakes of their imperfect but faithful parents:

May they be comforted in the knowledge that despite many worldly setbacks the Lord has been in control and there is now a blaze of gospel light in many dark places that will be remembered by multitudes of grateful saints for all eternity.

May there not be bitterness but rejoicing that comes from a humble and contrite heart, confident in this first promise of Jesus in His famous sermon: Blessed are the poor in Spirit for theirs is the

Kingdom of Heaven. (Matthew 5:3)

May we Mission Kids and our families all be held fast forever in His everlasting arms

Mission Kid brother, Ludin.

THANKS TO:

Peter Cooper, son of the BEM Mission Pilot, Ken Cooper, who later helped to train MAF pilot and author, Ron Watts and others. Thanks Peter for introducing us to modern Borneo and the SIB church blazing for Jesus there. Thanks for your encouragement and for allowing us access to BEM records for research and giving permission to share. Thanks to **Lyndale**, your beautiful Bornean wife, who is so grateful for the coming of the gospel that saved her and her people.

Paul Kerangkas, son of your legendary father Kerangkas, who faithfully supported my father through very tough times and sowed and watered much seed for Jesus. You do this too and have helped me appreciate the blazing work of the Spirit in northern Borneo. Your Dad would be proud that you are so faithful and true to Jesus. Eternity with mates like you will be awesome.

Libat and Anne Langub, our beautiful Kuching friends, so appreciative and faithful to BEM / SIB work. Thanks for showing us significant aspects of mission history and Bornean culture and sharing your own mission journey from subsistence village life to esteemed lawyer who loves Jesus – all because of BEM / SIB.

Doreen Battle, midwife and last surviving missionary of the final days of expatriate ministry in Ranau. You and your talented, multi-lingual and resilient, trekking pastor husband Wes, set BEM solidly on the commitment road to the SIB blaze that shines so strongly now as a tantalising epitaph of glorifying our King Jesus. Thanks to you both and to your lovely children and their families, still contending with the scars of all the sacrifice – your reward will be great in heaven. Chatting to you and praying about Borneo, Doreen, is like replaying a riveting adventure movie in Hi Fi. You open up news of the work and love of Jesus that makes my heart burn within.

Ray and Evelyn Cunningham, Sarawak missionaries who greatly supported my parents. At time of writing Ray is over 100 years old.

Many proof readers and encouragers have been behind the production of this book.

Thanks so much to you all:

My wife **Ellen**, Rev **Garry Dibley**, my brother **Chris** Ward, sister **Hilary** Williams, daughter **Christie,** ex KK Sabah school girl and retired, resourceful MK secretary to AFES, Moore College and the Anglican Schools Corporation **Elisabeth Arnett,** and **James**, **Nicole** and the team at Ark House Press, as well as all the other family and friends who have been supportive in us sharing the edifying news of the Gospel blaze in Borneo. Praise be to Jesus.

TABLE OF CONTENTS

PREFACE

"*Gospel Blaze in Borneo* brings back important memories of Jim Ward and his brother Chris when young, sons of missionary parents working in the 1950s for the Borneo Evangelical Mission (BEM) among the early believers in Ranau, situated below the famous Mount Kinabalu in Sabah.

Jim's trips back to Borneo, including this one with his wife, Ellen, in 2023, are like going back in time and into the future! The story of BEM bringing the saving power of Christ amongst the indigenous people in the interior of Sabah and Sarawak is truly amazing.

Looking back we can only say the story of BEM is ultimately "His Story". I believe the fascinating account by Jim in this book is going to be a great blessing to others."

(Libat Langub, legal advisor to BEM and beneficiary of a mission ministry that helped him on a huge journey from village subsistence living in the interior of Sarawak, to Melbourne University in Australia, to finally work as an esteemed lawyer in Kuching.)

May 2024

FOREWORD

In April 2023 Jim Ward, given the name of Ludin[*] by locals of Ranau, Sabah, Borneo, decided to revisit his missionary roots and took his wife Ellen for her first time visit to that alluring 'Land Below the Wind,' as Borneo became famously known back in the British colonial days. Jim and Ellen renewed exciting contact with Christian folk from fellowship groups founded by pioneer missionaries of the Borneo Evangelical Mission that began outreaching to Borneo in the late 1920s. The early missionaries are much revered today by Christians who have now spread throughout East Malaysia, which incorporates the two states of Sarawak and Sabah.

These missionaries include Jim's parents – James (Sabin) and Laura (Kumin) Ward, who worked in Ranau, Sabah, in the early 1950's not long after the atrocities of the Sandakan death marches that ended there in 1945

---

[*] It seems that the only mission children to be given native names were the four Ward children. Kumin was quite clear that native people chose names for them that they could say easily. It is noted that apart from James (Ludin) the three other English names are three syllables long and difficult for Dusuns to pronounce well. Also there are two in the family called James so the native names dispel any confusion and make things easy. The background story of how all this came about, though, remains a mystery!

with only six survivors. The war time starvation marches at the hands of merciless Japanese oppressors, surpassed the extent of the Burma Railway cruelties and were the single greatest atrocity perpetrated against Australians in the Second World War. But out of this terrible darkness has come the light of a wonderful indigenous church, called the Sidang Injil Borneo or SIB that has developed what the expatriate BEM church founders began.

Ellen and Jim discovered a thriving SIB Christian community stretching across East Malaysia that is non- denominational, biblically faithful, dynamic, culturally relevant and outreaching with an inspiring fervour of faith which is both inviting and challenging. It is totally self-supporting. The expatriate missionaries returned home in the 1970s but the light of the gospel now blazes brightly in Borneo.

Clockwise from top: Ludin atop of Sabin; Kumin; Kerangkas

CHAPTER ONE

Bon Voyage for Borneo.

When two seven-day Vacation Club gift accommodation certificates became available to us, we decided to combine them into a South East Asian adventure to explore Singapore and Malaysia. This seemed most appropriate for 70 years ago, in 1953, shortly after beginning my life in Hong Kong, I was flown by light aircraft into Ranau, Sabah, East Malaysia, where my parents, James and Laura worked as pioneer missionaries. They were called Sabin and Kumin by the local people they served. Here we settled on a cool, mountain plateau at the foot of the majestic Mt Kinabalu, Malaysia's highest mountain and third highest island peak on earth that rises abruptly to 13,435 feet from the narrow coastal plain, where the capital, Kota Kinabalu is situated. In those pre-independence days of the early fifties, Kota Kinabalu was called Jesselton and was an outpost of the British Empire. The interior was wild and undeveloped, with subsistence villages and long houses being the norm, and very few roads. Travellers just braved slippery tracks through thick mountainous jungle or boarded delicate river boats to traverse the mighty rivers and streams with their dangerous rapids and crocodiles in the estuaries.

One of the aims of this Borneo trip in April 2023, was to explore further my missionary background and give my wife, Ellen, a first experience of

Borneo, which is an alluring land, rich in fauna and culture. Its people are embracing the future with creative zest, and those in the interior have given up the vestiges of wild mid-nineteenth century witch-doctor culture and many are well educated. There has been a great turning to Christianity with a most impressive commitment and freedom from animistic superstition. We looked forward to visiting churches and learning from the faith and witness of fellow believers. I was last in Borneo in 1972 with my brother Chris, and then we climbed Mt Kinabalu with Paul, the son of my father's great helper, interpreter and trekker, Kerangkas. I had lost track of Paul but hoped we might meet again.

At first there were many preparation hurdles to overcome as well as mission contacts to line up. Then, just as we got underway it seemed like there were weird forces against us. My suitcase handle broke and then we discovered that the Sydney trains to the airport were all cancelled, where-upon my son Sam cheerfully informed me that troubles usually come in threes. We did not have long to wait before the next challenge arrived. Ellen was wearing a comfortable set of silk travelling slacks that I had not seen for quite some time. Unfortunately, the material set off the security alarms as we tried to get to our departure gate. She was tested repeatedly and on leaning over to look at the check screens, I was amazed to see large shapes that looked just like hand grenades and other weapons of considerable destruction hanging from her waist. This caused no small stir and supervisors scurried to where Ellen was now detained as the walkie talkies buzzed. I felt so sorry for my poor dear, as all her hand luggage and valuables went through the inspection area away from her but she could only stare mournfully at them and then at me. All was quickly resolved however as I retrieved the valuables and Ellen was quickly set free after a quick visit to a private, screened search area with a female pat down expert. Just the dress material! Note to self – it is always good to travel with someone else!

Letting down into the warm, still, tropical morning air over Kuching in Sarawak was like floating into an intriguing fairy land. Meandering rivers and sleepy fishing villages divide still significant tracts of jungle and arable plots that reach beyond subsistence now to cash crops of fruit and vegetables for the nearby towns. Nestled amongst this are low volcanic plugs that abruptly puncture the coastal plain with rugged castle like ramparts of mysterious allure. Later we were to find that many of these small peaks are shrouded in myth and legend. Way out north in the distance towards the South China Sea, National Parks of impressive forests and native fauna awaited our exploration. We were to be based for seven days at the restful resort of Damai Beach that has comfortable chalets right beside the calm waters and is overlooked by Mt Santubong. It is a full day's return climb to the summit on steep trails reminiscent of the Kokoda Track that I have enjoyed traversing twice with school groups.

Kuching is situated well inland, either side of the wide and winding Sarawak River. It is a bustling city of enterprising people of diverse means living in a wide variety of both rich and very poor, cramped accommodations. Our kind hosts – Libat and Anne - are energetic, intelligent Christians, who have successfully negotiated the transition from subsistence village life to tertiary studies and professional work in Kuching. Libat studied law at Melbourne University and has his own practice. They took us for a tasty Chinese meal and helped us acquire a hire car for the 30 kilometre trip out to Damai Beach Resort.

The serenity of Damai Beach was most welcome. Lush tropical vegetation, gurgling streams, cute little squirrels, palm trees laden with coconuts, and warm, calm, ocean swims worked their soothing magic, and it was wonderful to relax. Nearby is the Sarawak Cultural Village with representative native houses from the different tribal areas of Sarawak. A spectacular performance in colourful native costumes with traditional instruments and graceful dance moves, climaxed a most engrossing exposure to the impressive skills and inventions of indigenous Bornean culture. This included a blow pipe demonstration that was extremely dramatic and humbling as one realised the ingenuity that has allowed millions to survive down through the years without the benefit of the inventions of the west. Although the sadness of animistic superstition and head-hunting rituals entrapped most in olden times, it was good to see that faith in God has set many free to grow joyfully in doing what is right, exhibit compassion and to mature in service work to help others. Libat and Anne are good examples of this.

The coming of the missionaries brought education and insight and we were introduced to this at their Borneo Evangelical Mission (BEM) church, where the worship is varied, enticingly celebratory and overflowing with a powerful message of faith in Jesus. We were invited to a mid-week meeting to hear the history of the BEM, which was started by three Australians in 1928. One of these was Hudson Southwell, who trained in theology at the Melbourne Bible Institute, Australia, and whom Jim and Ellen met in Townsville in their university days in the early 1970s. At the mid-week BEM meeting we were delighted to meet a retired teacher by the name of Lim Siok Hong who was converted under Hudson's ministry and testified to the great witness and energetic work of the pioneer missionaries, who brought the gospel to both Sarawak and Sabah in East Malaysia.

The pioneers are regarded with the deepest respect by the Christian folk of this land, who are living proof of the fruit of brave Christian twentieth century outreach, which had to contend with the ravages of dissolute rice wine drunkenness, animistic customs, Japanese invasion in the Second World War and the political turmoil that followed. In the early fifties, my parents – James and Laura Ward- answered a mission call to the Ranau area near mighty Mt Kinabalu, inland from Kota Kinabalu in Sabah. We looked forward very much to visiting this area where they shared the gospel to native folk, who were without hope amidst their broken culture in the aftermath of the horrors of the Sandakan death march. Soon, many experienced the joy of Christianity and we hoped to meet some of their descendants.

We boarded our plane for Kota Kinabalu very happy and grateful for many pleasant Kuching walks, a fascinating museum visit, delicious fish meals in various seaside restaurants and an inspiring morning service at the BEM church – which is part of the East Malaysian SIB churches group. SIB stands for Sidang Injil Borneo and it was formed in 1959 and is a totally self - supporting indigenous church chain. The expatriate missionaries departed in the 1970s – their task is over.

Kota Kinabalu (KK) – or city of Mt Kinabalu – is set on a narrow coastal plain beside the South China Sea. It has a vigorous fishing fleet and the beautiful off shore islands are worth a visit. This city used to be called Jesselton when it was a British colony and that name was given to the small but stately hotel where we stayed. There we sampled the restrained but enticing opulence of the colonial days and were once more reunited with Libat and Anne from Kuching, who, fortuitously, were up on business. More SIB Christian folk came and met us and we were guided to a Christian village area to the south east where we heard great tales of families helping each other in gospel outreach and seeing much spiritual growth. This surpassed the dominant Moslem control that is general throughout Malaysia. After some very pleasant walks around KK, we readied our little hire car for the intended journey into the interior of North Borneo to Ranau and then across to Sandakan.

Mount Kinabalu can be seen as a distant, misty, massif from KK, but as you drive towards it, stupendous slabs of tortured rock rear up most dramatically to a series of jagged peaks that look like the broken jaws of a great shark. It is a two day arduous climb to the summit and my brother Chris and I completed this with Paul Kerangkas in 1972.

This car journey was inspiring as, in the clear dawn, from the Kinabalu pass we could see from one side of the island of Borneo to the other. No wonder this mighty mountain has become a universal symbol of divinity. I wondered what had happened to my old climbing friend Paul Kerangkas, as we had lost touch since those days in 1972 when we struggled to conquer the summit climb of this amazing mountain.

CHAPTER TWO

Hope Dawns Amidst Deep Despair.

The road into the interior is now sealed and very busy. Although the surface has many dips and buckles it is acceptable but the high speeds of traffic upon it can be disconcerting. Rounding a bend one can suddenly be forced swiftly to a crawl up steep grades behind trucks labouring to get their loads through the mountains to the plateau beyond. Natural human impatience often stimulates considerably risky manoeuvres executed with contemptuous aplomb by the drivers of fast SUVs and saloons. Heart rates leap up as vehicles surge suddenly ahead, to blind pass on hills or play havoc on the wrong side of the road into the face of oncoming traffic. Always above and around us though, the ramparts of Kinabalu dominate with their timeless, magnificent, calm majesty that is a powerful counterpoint to the scurrying of the ant like people below. The beauty of this highland scenery has always stood as a symbol of spiritual solace. It gives relief from reminders of the head hunting tortures of humanity that have plagued countless generations below its lofty peaks.

I wondered whether, at the end of the Second World War, this mountain idyll provided some refreshment to the poor, tattered remnants of allied POWs forced marched to their deaths from Sandakan to Ranau by cruel, merciless Japanese guards. There are many memorials of this barbaric, hopeless, destruction of thousands, which was only survived by six men. Those who did make it to Ranau had to carry heavy loads on starvation rations further into these very mountains until they dropped.

The BEM mission site in Ranau was obtained cheaply because it was the "blood ground" which no one wanted because the Japanese headquarters pursued relentless torture and massacre there. When they were finally defeated in 1945, Christian ministry was born with the coming of missionaries who made sacred this ground with news of the hope of the gospel of the love of Jesus. Hope dawned then for all - animistic tribes, ambitious imperialists and rebels fighting for the independent nation hood of Malaysia.

Jim's parents – Sabin and Kumin - were part of this Christian outreach in 1951 and when Jim arrived in 1953 to spend the first few years of his life in this much disputed territory, he was called Ludin and carried about by many of the now happy, native converts, who saw the fruit of what a Christian family really looked like. Jim was of the same stock as the POWs but born a generation later of an Australian engineer father and a British doctor mother. They both lived by faith, relying on God for everything they needed. They were very poor and sometimes just kept alive with food given out of the kindness of the new converts to Christianity. Their treasure was in heaven, however, and they practised much love and care that attracted many to the gospel. Their strong, confident, consistent Christian message that focused on the offer of the amazing grace for forgiveness of all sin for all who believed in Jesus, displayed a joyful freedom that was accompanied by medical help from Kumin and inventive assistance from Phd scientist Sabin.

As a radio physicist who had specialised in electrical engineering and the design of aerials during the Second World War, Sabin was ideally placed to set up a mission radio network and install engines in canoe conversions that made a big difference against the strong currents of the mighty rivers such as the Labuk, near Sandakan. The rivers were main transport routes through wild jungle at a time when there were no really serviceable roads and very few airstrips.

The boon of light aircraft was a massive help with small scale mission communication logistics and gathering new leaders to attend training camps. For regular outreach and nurture of new churches, however, foot slogging on treacherous trails and fighting dangerous river rapids was essential. Just before leaving the field in 1955 for Australia, Sabin, and Kumin, now pregnant with second son Chris (Andreas), bid an emotional farewell to the new church folk in Ranau and pioneered long house first contact outreach, along the Labuk River with support from Anglican missionaries at Sandakan. They were only in Ranau for one and a half years but the growth of Christianity during that time was spectacular. The fantastic spread of the gospel with new churches starting in these wild areas was a wonderful antidote to the nightmares of the war, especially the death marches.

The new Ward family of four enjoyed the luxury of the ship *Thorstrand* as it made for Sydney via Townsville in 1955, which was to be Kumin's first experience of Australia. Little did the couple realise then that they would return to Townsville in 1966. God would richly reward Sabin for forgoing his scientific career for four years to become a missionary. He would be appointed foundation Professor of Physics at James Cook University. Kumin was also rewarded as she started the health centre there on campus and was involved as the first woman on the council of Townsville Grammar School and the Committee that worked to set up the beautiful Good Shepherd Hospice for the elderly alongside the Ross River in Townsville.

Laura and James Ward enjoyed witnessing to students and colleagues alike in Townsville and were very glad to welcome Bornean visitors, including mission founders Hudson and Winsome Southwell who had two adopted indigenous children, Lukut and Mina. Many missionaries visited Sabin and Kumin and their growing progeny in a large home near the Strand – the Townsville beach front. Some amazing Bornean tale telling and considerable rejoicing took place over many years. Four Ward children grew up as Queenslanders but were taken on several visits back to Borneo to stay in Ranau for vacation. The delighted Ranau church folk gave them all native names to establish identity and relationship: Ludin (Jim), Andreas, (Chris), Rudi (Alistair) and Lantana (Hilary). Each of these second generation mission kids has embraced a Christian faith-walk and are symbols of the many jewels with which God has covered the old debris of war time death.

Hearing our Ranau contacts speak with reverence of the post- Second World War work, it was hard to take in all at once the extent and exciting rush of those brief pioneering years, when the harvest of souls was so rich. It was good for stability amidst all this to focus on the ethereal Kinabalu Mountains above. Reflection helped us realise the miracle of a whole people coming to believe that Mt Kinabalu, once the sacred heaven of the old spirit believers, was actually created by the one Almighty God who truly loved them, and had called them to build churches in the valleys below. Now, instead of mountain spirits, they worshipped Jesus, their new friend who had given them access to God's Holy Spirit, far more powerful than any witch doctor's demons. With a new found freedom from animistic fear, they joyfully shared the gospel of God's enormous gift of eternal life to all who believed in Him. This gospel sharing began to blaze like a wild fire.

It was only on this trip that Jim came to realise that his 1953 blond-haired contented baby persona, as little Ludin amongst a people, still weeping from wicked spirits and bloodletting, was actually a symbol for many of the birth of a new, fulfilling culture. Now there was hope of a joyous future – new life, all one with Jesus in the jungle. Young Ludin began to walk on the Ranau airstrip amidst people who were also learning to walk with Jesus as they quickly laboured to put old habits away and love each other after seasons of sin and superstitious hate. New infants, well cared for, became important symbols of a whole people learning to walk in contrite innocence with Jesus their new King.

The gratitude of the new church descendants to all the pioneer missionaries and their children has been wonderful. All are welcomed and treated with enormous respect and intensely genuine care and hospitality. The Sidang Injil Borneo (SIB) church is a totally self-supporting beacon of hope throughout East Malaysia now, but its BEM roots are still much revered. Just before the Easter weekend on Thursday 6 April 2023, as we descended from the high pass around Kinabalu to the plateau of the Ranau plain, we realised that mighty Kinabalu had become a symbol for a new building of faith on the great rock of the Father who never fails. We did not anticipate, however, the coming beautiful outpouring of loving thanks that we were about to experience from many Christian folk, now prospering in walks of joy with Jesus.

CHAPTER THREE

The Road to Sandakan.

Half way down to Ranau we stopped at the beautiful mountain village of Kundasang, which is the tourist jumping off point for Mt Kinabalu expeditions and tours. There to meet us was our cheerful host, Lui, a retired Christian policeman who lives there and, we were to find, assists in a fine little church with a great view over the town built in the steep mountain hills and valleys. He bore great news for us. Paul Kerangkas, son of Kerangkas, famed early church leader and great shepherd of many new Christian flocks, who assisted Sabin in mission trekking and evangelism and church growth in the pioneering days, was now living back in Ranau, close to what has become a very large and vibrant church there. He would be waiting for us as we passed through on our trip to Sandakan. This was a great thrill.

Well, we got a little lost driving into Ranau as the google maps confused us a bit and the town is so built up now, but soon, after we had circled through the large bustling shopping centre, we found the intersection marked by a statue of a fish and right there was the church and Paul Kerangkas waiting to meet us with a firm, friendly handshake. What joy.

Paul Kerangkas is so healthy, happy and well, enjoying farming near Ranau and supporting Christian folk with a fervour that does credit to his famous father. Soon we were walking together to the two remaining rain trees of three planted by my father near what was then a simple wood and thatch open sided Ranau church building. Now, it has been replaced by a large modern concrete church building that is still being extended as so many come to service there. The rain trees have grown massive and symbolise the mighty growth of the Christian churches in this region.

We were to find out that now there are sixty satellite churches in the neighbouring villages. Many have turned to Christ. Faith was exercised, even 'as small as a mustard seed,' and now - mountains have moved. It was exciting to talk with Paul beneath the comfort of these trees, planted by my father seventy years ago, and then bow our heads to read the memorial right there of the end of the death marches on this very spot. Where there were the horrors of hatred there is now faith, love and much care for any seeker, regardless of cultural background.

With hearts full of fresh insights to God's many blessings, we continued easterly towards Sandakan for a two night stay, promising to return to Ranau for church service on Easter Sunday, 2023.

It is a tortuous five hour journey across the top of Borneo to Sandakan. Lumpy, pot holed bitumen, slow village transport, zooming four wheel drives and many roadworks all command close attention. This vital transport route bisects vast expanses of palm oil plantation on the undulating plain. We stayed at the pleasant Elopuro hotel right on the Sandakan waterfront. Elopuro, the original name for Sandakan, means "beautiful town" and this bustling city, once the capital of North Borneo, is set along the coast of a huge sheltered waterway and port. It is most scenic. There are always ships and fishermen to gaze at and small fast launches ply about on countless mysterious missions in all directions. We enjoyed a cool coke and tasty meal at a waterfront café amidst the Ramadan night life of hordes of people satisfying their hunger after sunset at myriads of temporary street food booths, before settling into happy groups of family and friends.

A strong logging industry, much trade and a secure harbour with many little outlying villages, have always made Sandakan a popular stop for shipping from around the world. Almost in sight are the outlying islands of the Philippines to the north east, infamous for pirates who traditionally have raided Borneo. Super powers to the north, west and south make Sandakan the mysterious fulcrum for the swinging sweep of the whole of South East Asia. A free, politically stable Sandakan is a natural buffer between the encroaching sea power of an increasingly aggressive China and the settled sprawl of the mighty archipelagos of Indonesia, the Solomons and New Guinea.

Sandakan became famous internationally through the writings of Agnes Keith, American wife of a British government official stationed here in the halcyon last days of the British Empire. Agnes arrived in 1934 and wrote whimsically with a fine eye for amusing detail of the various tribal interactions and customs colliding with British expatriate opulence, in what she called *The Land Below the Wind*. This is the evocative title of her first novel of three that record her suffering under Japanese occupation and return to assist restoration of Sandakan, which was destroyed in the Second World War.

Ellen and I enjoyed a splendid morning exploring the Keith's fully restored old Colonial house and beautiful grounds, set high on a hill overlooking the harbour to catch the serene, gentle tropic sea breezes. Agnes and her husband finally left Sandakan just before my parents arrived in 1951. Just before they left in 1955, they were to use it as a base for evangelism north and inland on the mighty Labuk River.

Juxtaposed with this enchanting tourism was a most salutary visit to the Sandakan POW camp site. The memorial gardens there are beautifully landscaped and cared for with many inscriptions and displays that confront every visitor with the horrors of savage incarceration, which ended with the forced death marches between 1942- 1945. Thousands died all the long weary way back to Ranau. The enormity of this was a slap in the face as I stood at the gate from which they turned left and west to a gruelling and desperate destruction, of which most were unsuspecting. The memorial gardens are well labelled with the essential facts, which, together with detailed internet records, provide trustworthy sources for this reflection.

Strangely, it seems that there were allied scouting missions by Z Force special unit to consider a rescue of the POWs in Sandakan. A rescue mission, dubbed Operation Kingfisher, was planned and trained for, but Australian generals procrastinated on any action, citing lack of support from the Americans. The attempted rescue raid was called off on 19 April 1945, when it was wrongly reported that there were no POWs left in camp. It is hard to believe that the intelligence gathering was so pitiful. The impetus for POW rescue in Borneo, which might easily have become an expensive invasion, got lost amidst the rocky landscape of overbearing American leadership that called all the shots in the allied ranks, afflicted still with a shocked, defensive mentality. It took a fatally long while for the allies to countenance the growing, demoralising, and horrifying realisation that the Japanese planned to massacre all POWs at the end of the war.

Not many Americans were involved. So, several thousand Australian and British troops of the lower ranks died cruelly, whilst the Americans slipped over to invade the Philippines, seeking the flash of glory of Macarthur's promised return, which occurred on October 20 1944. This is where the fighting focus went into 1945, before the atomic bombs pre-empted further POW massacre throughout the entire region.

Along the tedious drive back to Ranau, through the endless palm oil plantations, one is assailed with nightmares of the massive challenge of marching all this way without food or rest. It is a miracle that some POWs ever made it to Ranau in their starved, emaciated state. Now, just like Kokoda Track journeys, there are tours that walk in the footsteps of these brave forbears and hallow the ground where they sacrificed for their country.

The last camp site on this expedition walk is on the outskirts of Ranau and at the Ranau SIB church, there is now a small museum of artefacts and displays that record the final massacres. This dignifies the appalling sacrifice with hope that it was not in vain and that we have all learned positive lessons from it about the crucial importance of multicultural caring. Just beside the museum are Sabin's rain trees and the wonderful non-denominational SIB church, now spawning many satellite worship places that stand firm as Christian beacons of hope. This is a healing balm to the stark horror of the records that show that just six men survived out of 1,496 Australian and 1,004 British POWs, who left Sandakan to march to their cruel deaths – shot, beaten and otherwise murdered - in the treacherous jungle ramparts towards Mt Kinabalu.

After all this sadness that was a dominant focus for us in Sandakan, it was a relief to see again the lofty grandeur of Mt Kinabalu and remember that the next day was Easter Sunday 2023. We planned to worship with many brothers and sisters in the place where my parents helped share gospel joy amidst the post war paralysis of poverty, moral shock and secretive guilt, occasioned by such savage inhumanity.

CHAPTER FOUR

Renewal at Ranau.

A few times in the life of most Christians there are special days that stand out for an incredibly uplifting focus that echoes the great heavenly feast with Jesus that all believers are promised to share in one day on His triumphant return. Perhaps one might point to a memorable wedding, or an inspiring memorial address or a new era leadership talk or the reuniting of separated loved ones. Easter Sunday 9 April 2023 became one of those days for us as guests of the Christian folk in Ranau. We were thoughtfully provided with interpreters and our every need was met.

In one glorious day, during which we seemed to be blessed with added fortitude that many back home in Australia were praying for us, we breakfasted with the Ranau church leaders, worshipped with an inspiring sermon interpreted for us in the main Ranau church, and then journeyed to the large satellite church of Bongkud for more worship, communion and lunch. After this we visited the Namaus bible school campus of the impressive Borneo Theological Seminary for afternoon tea, and then Camp Bongkud which provides an authentic village living experience for groups from all over the world. Nearby we viewed houses built under the supervision and assistance of the great missionary shepherd Trevor White, who is honoured by a photographic display in the local community hall. Following this we journeyed back into the Kinabalu area with Lui to his Kundasang church for a special evening welcome worship time at which I spoke and Paul Kerangkas interpreted, just as his father had done for my father nearly 70 years ago.

My message was sparked by the symbol of the rain trees – just as a small planting by Sabin on the fearful killing fields has now left us with two massive trees for all to see and take shelter under, so the gospel of Jesus has taken amazing root and grown to over sixty churches in the whole Ranau area. Now peace and love prevail. Tribal differences and payback despair, pillage and torture of cruel invaders, superstition and the suffocating blanket of much fear over all Borneo are replaced by a glorious unity of brothers and sisters in God's family of love and care.

This Christian love stretches around the world and definitely back to Australia, England and other 'home countries' and even in a new ally - Japan, where there is much forgiveness and ongoing mission work. Old pioneer Bornean missionaries rejoice from afar, despite declining physically, for their difficult job has been well done and at just the right time there comes the reward of triumphant rest with our dear Saviour, King Jesus. In Him Christian folk will be forever united with all believers of all time from every culture.

In the meantime, the company of the Firstborn from death can delight in being entrusted with the stupendous enterprise of guiding more and more people towards this transcendent Kingdom of their beloved Jesus. What a Kingdom! It is the safest and most joyous of harbours, the ultimate haven from the hell of evil. In the Kingdom of Jesus there is forgiveness. We are washed spotlessly clean of all sin, and all the weaknesses of self are addressed perfectly by the Holy Spirit.

One of the most remarkable features of this Easter Sunday for me was observing and experiencing the joy of what I have called enlightened syncretism: the miraculous weaving of a brand new multi-cultural non-denominational church out of the examples of many church traditions from both east and west, old and new. In Ranau now there is dynamic preaching, which is confidently biblical, extempore and fluent. It is supported with a rich repertoire of old and new Christian music sung to lively rock bands, with the drummer expertly housed behind acoustic perspex! Universal is the imaginative use of electronics and computer screens. At only two to three generations downstream from simplistic village animism this is all most impressive.

We felt immediately at home in a genuinely familiar worship context, which was not just a western culture copy. There was more that impressed - the dancing. Tasteful, magnificently but modestly and immaculately dressed dancers sway reverently to familiar songs and contribute some percussion that enhances reverence and does great credit to graceful native Bornean long house music traditions of the past.

Wise eldership has rejected all pretention and unnecessary ceremony but nurtured respectful, enthusiastic, inspiring, worship that always focuses clearly on Jesus and His way of salvation. Doctrine is clear and pure but unobtrusive, allowing a high priority to be placed on parabolic teaching and rich testimony. These are greatly treasured. There are both women and men pastors who, although revered and adored by their flocks, persevere most humbly as servants, incessantly pointing people to Jesus and exhorting all to look towards hope in heaven. Pastoral care is taken very seriously and shared diligently by the elders.

Easter Sunday 2023 was like a beautiful, heavenly dream for us that easily bridged cultural difference and kept surprising with delightful insights to do with the growth of Kingdom unity and self-sacrifice. This kept jumping from the present to the past and then bravely on into long term future planning. Time really did seem to stand still. Fellowship with all at Ranau was cheerful, joyous and openly honest and transparent. Ellen was struck by the age diversity and large numbers at these gatherings as well as the welcoming generosity of all. The great love, care and thoughtfulness given to children's ministries was also impressive.

There is an inspiring and instructive vision here that needs our prayers to protect. The Bongkud church folk come from a very poor subsistence past that was alleviated to a large extent by the practical ministry of missionary Trevor White with his sawmill and carpentry. Paul Kerangkas said that he never knew how to use a hammer until Trevor White taught him! Bongkud Christians began to prosper. They continue to live in modest circumstances but now they are all working together to build a huge new church building to replace the old one that they have outgrown. Faith and love are clearly manifest in the midst of these happy people, and one senses the climate of the early church, where everything was held in common to benefit all.

We should pray that this is kept unspoilt in Borneo, which is afflicted by the trappings of materialism and where there are bribes from other dominant faith groups, willing to pay good money and provide lucrative jobs for young folk who renounce Christianity. It is opportune to pray that every soldier of Christ here will count the cost of foregoing worldly wealth as nothing beside the acquisition of 'the pearl without price' – the eternal Kingdom of Jesus.

Other denominationally based missionaries reached in towards the interior a bit from the East Coast, notably those working for the Sandakan Bethel Mission and then the Anglican Church. The wonderful story of CMS missionary, school teacher Sylvia Jeanes from Queensland working under Walter Newmarch up to Tongud along the Kinabatangan River from 1967, has been well told in the biography about her called *Riding the Rapids**. Her

---

* *Riding the Rapids, The Story of Sylvia Jeanes* by Ashleigh Hooker, CMS / SPCK Australian Publishing 2007.

commitment also saw substantial spiritual fruit as many turned to Christ while her expatriate colleagues were sent home. She, however, gained great respect of the civil authorities who finally granted her permanent residency and she settled in Kota Kinabalu. The SIB/BEM work is notable however in being better set up for self-sufficiency because it is non– denominational and not overtly identified with western Christian tradition. Being self-supporting it is therefore free to develop its own culturally relevant training and governance. Whatever the conduit though, the Holy Spirit has blazed forth so that the gospel has been expressed to Borneans in clear terms. All the Christian proclamations have been precious.

Late that Sunday night, Paul Kerangkas drove us back to our little hire car left near the rain trees and we nosed cautiously out into a dark night to return to our country area Homestay. It was very dark and not easy to find our way, but I was reminded amidst the vibrancy and Easter light of this day's joyous memories, that my parents had also experienced darkness in Ranau but had persevered with many others, so that now multitudes enjoy the rich legacy of a wonderful Christian family here. Despite the work of evil in this land, John 1: 4 -5 remains true to spur us all on in faith:

"In Jesus was life, and that life was the light of all mankind. The light shines in the darkness, and the darkness has not overcome it."

CHAPTER FIVE

Running the Race of Perseverance.

On Easter Monday we drove around to the large comfortable house of Paul Kerangkas, not far from the rain trees, to say goodbye. We met his lovely, humble, wife Dorothy and son Luther, who trained in Russia for seven years to be a doctor! Paul and Dorothy also have three daughters. Paul's kind, gentle brother Maibul was also there. In 1981 he drove my visiting parents and sister Hilary (Lantana) all the way from Ranau to Kota Kinabalu on the coast just to catch the plane home. Quite a journey and not something one would normally impose on an acquaintance. Maibul remembers their visit well with fondness and again I marvelled at how barriers of distance, culture and personal reticence are swept aside in God's Kingdom.

We found out that Paul's father Kerangkas died back in 2013, at the same time that my father passed on in Australia. I am sure that their heavenly trekking will be most joyous and they will be deeply fulfilled by the fruit of their ministry in Sabah. Sadly we had just missed Paul's mother, who had recently gone home to be with Jesus and meet her husband.

God had another surprise in store for me. Living next door to Paul and also present for morning tea, was Muriam, Paul's sister. We were amazed to learn that when she was five years old she used to help look after me - little baby Ludin in 1954. Now it was 2023! She remembers well my parents and all the tempestuous years of the growing Ranau church. She told me that I was a bit naughty and liked to chase all the valuable chickens! She, with many others in Ranau, has learned through many ups and downs to remain faithful to Jesus, as I have tried to learn in Australia. Now, after all these years, we are reunited, brother and the kind sister I never knew I had. I was stunned by the reach of God's family in both time and place.

There were photographs and prayers together, followed by a quick trip to the overgrown Ranau airstrip, now decommissioned. Here I had learned to walk. Later I had to learn to walk the 'talk' with Jesus and this has been going on for seventy years, despite some shaky steps. From this airstrip, mission planes and later regular air transport carried my parents and many other missionaries and their families in and out of Ranau, fulfilling a vital support ministry. The short Ranau grass airstrip has served its purpose and now communications are maintained with fast cars on bitumen roads east and west.

Some aviation essence must have clung to me from my babyhood, however, as aircraft have always been an inspirational pursuit of mine and it has been a great joy that the Lord enabled me to gain my private pilot's licence with an instrument rating, share ownership of a Mooney 201 plane for a while and fly it to many parts of Australia. My flying training was put to good use with the Outback Patrol organisation led by Les Nixon, and it was most rewarding to fly puppeteers from Quizworks to small towns with their tiny schools in outback NSW and Queensland.

The time of the expatriate, skilled missionaries has well and truly gone. A new era of indigenous outreach, growth and discipleship has dawned, but it is stabilised and built on solid foundations laid by the Borneo Evangelical

Mission pioneers. They bravely confronted animism and shared the gospel light, fanning it into flame by translating the scriptures into local languages, sweating and suffering disease alongside the native people on massive preaching treks, as they shared vital life survival skills with new converts who were most apprehensive about renouncing witchdoctors and their suffocating charms.

Missionaries, especially from Australia and the UK, returned to serve the people despite bitter memories of the Second World War savagery of the death marches. Their witness prevailed, undergirded always by the incredible power of the Holy Spirit who helped to overcome every flaw and false direction as many throughout the world prayed. Satan has tried very hard to extinguish this flame but God's Spirit has consecrated, counselled and comforted at every turn, so that he has been thwarted.

Now the Ranau church is the nucleus for over sixty churches, some very small village meeting places, others large, like the massive Bongkud organisation, but all are webbed together in non-denominational accord with a vision that makes one gasp, before bursting into praise of our great God.

To this day Ellen and I remain deeply challenged by all this to consider our own gospel outreach at home. Is it keeping up with the massive spawning of our new Western Sydney suburbs and the weird demographics of our own syncretic, multicultural and materialistic times? There is much wisdom, courageous faith, vision and insight that Bornean Christians can teach us if we are humble enough to learn, free of pretention, racial intolerance and the dominance of the materialistic greed that threatens to compromise us.

The sun came out that Easter Monday and it really did seem that Mt Kinabalu was smiling at us with a crystal clear glory as we wound our way west around her glowing, magnificent, rugged ramparts and dropped into the peak hour traffic jams of Kota Kinabalu. So many splendid cars now buzz to a standstill around the city, where we lost count of the number of Kentucky Fried Chicken franchises.

Ensconced in a comfortable Hotel near the airport where my brother Alistair – Rudi - used to land when he piloted jets there for Malaysian Airlines in the 1990s, we could still see Kinabalu in the distance from our room. Now her majestic silhouette symbolised a bold new commitment vision for us to transcend the bustle to get rich. We must remember the lessons of the Ranau SIB church to lay up treasure in heaven, not here in the materialism of this troubled planet that is fatally plagued by the "god of this world." We pray that we might have the wisdom and self-sacrifice to embrace the call of the King to take up our cross and follow Him.

The next day we were to fly out for Singapore and the tests to treading the narrow path of faith, would begin again, coming from many different directions. For now, Kinabalu was a mountain of great hope in an eternal cross-cultural future, and she farewelled us with an ethereal lightshow of dazzling tropic sky hues at both sunset and then again with the sun rising over its craggy tops in the early morning of our departure from Borneo.

It only takes a spark to get a fire going but as the old gospel song says – 'all those around will warm up to its glowing and that's how it is with God's love once you have experienced it.' This trip to Borneo certainly challenged Ellen and I about whether our gospel light is shining brightly with the hope of treasure in heaven. We reaffirmed our need to blaze for Jesus whilst we can – so many around need to experience the glorious love and hope of God.

On the visit to Borneo in 1972 when my brother Chris and I climbed Mt Kinabalu together with Paul Kerangkas, the young people's fellowship leaders of the open sided thatched roofed Ranau church of that time, came across the paddock beside the rain trees - small in those days - to what is now the pastor's house, where we were staying for Christmas and New Year. They asked if Ludin would come and speak words of encouragement to their group!

I had never preached a sermon before but one of the advantages of speaking through an interpreter is that you get a few moments to collect your thoughts before each new utterance. I shared one of my favourite passages – Hebrews Chapter 12:1 – 11 about following Jesus, the Firstborn King, who has carved a path of light out of the dark chaos of a fallen world and calls on us all to lay aside all distraction and sin and run the race of faith along this path with perseverance, looking always towards Him and the great prize of a large cross cultural Christian family sharing His glorious eternity. This message was warmly received and there we were, young Christian brothers and sisters, joyously one in Christ, encouraging each other to apply this teaching in our lives ahead, despite massively diverse racial, economic and cultural backgrounds.

Typical of scripture, Hebrews 12:1-13 has never dated and seems a most apt way to sum up this tale of two Aussies travelling to explore Borneo in 2023. Little did I know as the youth Ludin in that single little open sided wooden Ranau church talk of 1972, and speaking of following Jesus on the very ground where the blood of many of my Aussie forbears was spilt in horrible agony just 37 years earlier, that the spark lit by the pioneer missionaries with the help of that same Jesus would become an amazing blaze in Borneo that continues to obliterate the dark despair of hatred and materialistic oblivion today. Now, gentle, kind and caring people walk tall and free from superstition and violence, without the help of the west. There is no greater proof of the authenticity of the gospel than this.

And so we pray that always we will all look to Jesus, the pioneer and perfecter of our faith, and, as we accept His discipline of us as beloved children, never waver or stumble in our work and witness for Him.

CHAPTER SIX

Undergirded by the Prayers of Many Saints

One of the great miracles of Christian outreach in every corner of the world in both the present and for the future, is that every Christian brother and sister of any background, ability level and gifting can participate in the mission of advancing the gospel by praying to our dear Father in the powerful name of the Firstborn- Jesus.

The whole mission outreach of the Bornean Evangelical Mission and the ongoing work of the Sidang Injul Borneo has been and is still undergirded by the fervent prayers of a whole army of saints. The missionaries in the front line of call and proclamation are the visible tip of a mighty intercession of many invisible but faithful believers and supporters for Kingdom success. Great is the rejoicing of these multitudes, when there is a blaze of Gospel light after the invisible army is able to witness a tremendous answer to their many consistent and faithful intercessions. They are finally able to rejoice in seeing false pathways rejected and the fire of God's Spirit being fanned into much new birth and revival of faith in Jesus.

God listens and blesses such faith and belief for that is what pleases Him. (Hebrews 11: 1) Thanks be to God for those who have, and still today, take time and make the effort – sometimes to the point of "sweating blood" - to support mission in focused, fervent prayer that looks faithfully and earnestly to results that glorify the Father. They will all be blessed, especially when Jesus returns.

We are promised in Romans 8:26-27 that God's Spirit intercedes and helps us with this with 'groaning too deep for words'. We do not have to be great speakers, just faithful servants who work at getting into and staying in the habit of daily specific conversation with their master that includes asking Him to strengthen, encourage and equip those both near and far away, who are engaged in Gospel outreach.

Great Christian leaders give us a fine example of being prayer warriors for Jesus. They show us that the prayer support needs to be habitual, ongoing and may stretch for a lifetime for some special situations. The point of mentioning the following few praying saints is that, although all passed on now, they are well known for having been very busy Christians in extremely responsible positions but they still humbly made the time to pray for Sabin and Kumin in Borneo as well as many other missionaries needing support. They model the commitment and hard work needed for prayer so that gospel light will blaze. God has chosen to work though us and nurture our faith in this way and we need to embrace His perfect will.

Laura's home church whilst she was training in London to be a doctor during the Second World War, was All Souls Langham Place where a young pastor by the name of John Stott was just beginning his amazing career as one of the world's best Christian teachers and writers. John took a special interest in encouraging Laura, when he realised that she was considering missionary work and especially when her new Aussie fiancé, James, and the Borneo destination came into view. John faithfully prayed for the whole four years of the Sabin and Kumin Bornean outreach and then continued this for the Ward family for all his life. He took an informed interest in the careers of each of the four children and later, whilst Ludin was post graduate studying at Regent College, Vancouver, wondering what his career should be, John Stott calmed Ludin's anxieties about growing up in the shadow of his talented parents and encouraged him to trust God one step at a time. John Stott visited the family in Townsville in the 70s. It was a joyous time, with much praise for God's faithfulness in Borneo as well as some outreach to James Cook University campus and a little tropical bird watching.

A letter dated 20 July 1951 from Sabin to the BEM Field Chairman, Alan Belcher in Lawas HQ, Sarawak, sheds interesting light on the energetic, faithful and visionary support for missionary work and the BEM in particular by the then largely unknown John Stott. Stott had just officiated in marrying Jim and Laura on the 30 June 1951 at All Souls Church. Jim writes to Borneo three weeks later from the ship *Carthage* on the way to the mission field:

"The South East Asia Prayer Group of the C of E All Souls Langham Place (a key evangelical C of E in London) has adopted the China Inland Mission and the Borneo Evangelical Mission and are praying regularly for the work. Just before sailing the Vicar (Rev John Stott MA) advised that they are making available 45 pounds sterling for our equipment and general mission use. This is indeed encouraging and we believe that the interest will continue."

(BEM letters 1951)

This is a most generous donation for the time and underlines the great truth that the front line of mission work stands very much on the shoulders of those supporting from behind. All Christians can and should be involved in mission. Rev John Stott married Sabin and Kumin, organised solid prayer and financial support for them and then followed up over many years. This is most impressive but indicative of counting the cost of mission 'at home as well as abroad.'

While Sabin was studying in London, immediately post war, he was encouraged in his quest to be a missionary to Borneo by Christians from Australia visiting UK for conferences and academic study. They also undertook to pray for the Borneo outreach with the BEM. This has and is all bearing much fruit to this very day.

These "mates from Australia" included inveterate champion of world evangelical mission, Archbishop of Sydney and Anglican primate of Australia, Howard Mowll and his wife, Dorothy; Canon Thomas C Hammond, who, as Principal of Moore Theological College, Sydney, helped reset Sydney Anglicans on an evangelical footing, Archbishop Donald Robinson, who promoted the crucial priority of biblical preaching and Canon Stanley Kurrle, later a most successful caring, insightful headmaster of The King's School, Parramatta, under whom Ludin served for seven years as an English teacher. Stan was also intensely interested in using aviation for outreach and shared ownership of that Mooney 201 with Ludin during the 1980s.

These diverse but gifted supporters of BEM work were all photographed together with James at an Intervarsity Fellowship, conference in Swanwick, UK in 1948, just after Howard Mowll had been elected Primate of Australia. An irresistible confidence, gentle humour and courage shines out as they stand together to witness for Christ to the ends of the earth, just three years after the Ranau massacre of thousands of their countrymen. What godly soldiers of Christ, who were servant masters of contrition, vision, mercy and forgiveness.

The Australian 'Jungle' Doctor, Dr Paul White, ex missionary to Africa, was also a great prayer warrior for the Bornean outreach and a personal friend of Sabin. In 1975, Paul White greatly encouraged me when I was a travelling staff worker for the Australian Fellowship of Evangelical Students. Later, he visited the Ward family home in Townsville on his honeymoon with his new wife, Ruth. Sabin hosted them aboard his new little sloop,

Siang (Malayan for "light") for tropical sailing around Magnetic Island. This little yacht was to be greatly used in Christian fellowship outings in the tropics. After refurbishment it is still being used by Ludin, cruising, now in Sydney waters, as it continues a ministry of assisting Christian outreach and nurture.

The soldiers of Christ theme was most prominent in 1950s mission outreach. In the same letter previously quoted, Sabin says:

"Just before leaving (England for Borneo) we received a cable from the Home Council: '*Swords Drawn up to the Gates of Heaven.*' This was a fine thought from Melbourne and sent us on our way rejoicing." (BEM letters 1951)

What emerges from these reflections is that many different prayer warriors undergird resilient witness ensuring that it is empowered by the Holy Spirit but in doing so God uses them to create a rich tapestry of encouraging relationships. These inspire both those on the mission field interface and their supporters back home, as well as others around the world considering their gospel outreach.

It is both mysterious and joyous to experience the incredible power of the Holy Spirit sweeping through lost people and transforming them to be God's disciples, in the wake of really focused prayer by humble, righteous, committed saints. Australians sponsored the original outreach to Borneo from 1928 but are kept very humble as they realise the fruit of nearly a century of ministry now can reach back to challenge and encourage them. Three Aussies went out to Borneo to start the BEM, girded by the prayers of many, but now there is a multitude of SIB Bornean brothers and sisters who can deftly defy pretentious materialism and spiritual apathy and pray for gospel outreach in Australia, amidst its multicultural but compromised wealth seeking society, that is nevertheless searching for worthwhile roots.

CHAPTER SEVEN

First Contact Evangelism - Sharing Jesus Love along the Labuk River.

Sabin, like the other pioneer missionaries, quickly saw the need to use rivers for evangelisation trips. Soon after arriving in Ranau in 1952, Sabin and Kumin reached out into the wild interior along the upper reaches of two gigantic rivers flowing east to massive estuaries south and north of Sandakan. The banks of both rivers were densely, vegetated by thick, almost impenetrable rainforest, much of which has been cleared today to the detriment of the environment. To the south is the Kinabatangan River, which at 560 km long is Malaysia's second longest river after the Rajang River in Sarawak. To the north the Labuk River flows more directly East from near Ranau for a while before veering sharply north and then east and south again just north of Sandakan. Both rivers were important transport routes.

Other Christians such as the Roman Catholic and Anglican denominations with Walter Newmarch and Sylvia Jeanes began working in the more accessible Kinabatangan area but the Labuk was untouched and in great need of first contact for Jesus. Sabin saw this as his frontier calling.

There were many longhouse villages on the banks of the Labuk only accessed in those days of isolation by riding dangerous rapids in riverboats called jongkongs or negotiating some very rough jungle tracks that required considerable physical fitness. There were no roads and torrential rain made the cost of such infrastructure prohibitive. Many rapids and swift currents, especially in the wet season, made the Labuk extremely dangerous, just like most of the Bornean Rivers. Often huge logs came roaring down to smash away jetties, and flash floods drove people to rush for whatever scant higher ground there was, where they could be marooned in stilt houses for weeks. Starvation and disease were a constant threat.

Mission co – founder, Hudson Southwell, told the missionaries in his October 1951 report to them, of a village in Sarawak with hard resistant people asking him to leave as they feared that their ministry was causing evil spirits to afflict them with tremendous rains which caused abnormal flooding. Hudson and his friends retreated to a boat and got to a little palm house on the river banks where they thought that they would safe. They were marooned there for six days with their rice running low and then they had to get back into the boat as the water covered the house. He said that "it seemed that defeat had come." They persisted though, and the floods diminished and they returned to the resistant village, which eventually asked him to come and teach them about Jesus. The village people, along with quite a few other villages, saw the calm, confident faith of the missionaries and all turned to serve the Lord. With first contact stories like this fresh in their minds Sabin and Kumin focused on the Labuk River.

In contrast to this realism, we find as we read sources such as the Globerovers Magazine of July 2019, a more romantic, civilised contemporary view of

Bornean Rivers that appeals. The Bornean rainforest is "one of the oldest in the world …with over 1600 known species of animals, birds, amphibians and reptiles. The jungle is an Eden like paradise." The quaint and quirky Proboscis monkey is a great drawcard for tourists and today there is a sanctuary for them at the mouth of the Labuk near Sandakan. Such protection is crucial now, however, for rapid deforestation and the encroachment of oil palm plantations has "caused massive habitat destruction and pushed many species to the brink of destruction. Among the animals of Sabah under threat are the proboscis monkey, orangutan, clouded leopard, Bornean rhino, Bornean pygmy elephant, slow loris and the binturong bearcat."

(Globerovers Magazine 2019)

In the days of the Sabin and Kumin 1950s outreach, though, the Labuk wove dangerously through lush, impenetrable rainforest and the people had had little or no contact with any Christians bearing the good news of the love of Jesus. It was a totally wild frontier in which Sabin always carried firearms and his trekking, often with trusted pioneer guides Kerangkas and Kentuni, was characterized by high and sustained levels of alertness for many perils. There were continual frustrations such as the swarms of leaches, whose thick bloated bodies had to be removed from bloody socks at the end of a day's hike, and boat capsizes in which it was almost impossible to protect valuables such as cameras. Also, many village dogs would always seem to howl just at the time in the evenings when Sabin and Kerangkas would begin gospel talks in the longhouses. The rule of the evil spirits and witchdoctors was often violently apparent and spawned much deep anxiety and opposition. Tribal conflict was rife and drunkenness was the pervasive antidote for many desperate and lost indigenous people.

Sabin, however, was encouraged by the stories of God powerfully at work along the rivers in Sarawak and saw immediately the vast potential for outreach along the Labuk. On an exploratory trip in early 1953, Sabin and Kumin witnessed encouraging awakening as some villagers responded positively to the gospel. The couple returned from this reconnoitre excited and challenged by this. They got back to Ranau just in time to go on leave to Hong Kong for the birth of Ludin, their first son. Some Labuk villagers had welcomed the missionaries and listened carefully to the gospel message; others said that they would obey their witchdoctors and they asked the missionaries to leave. Battle lines were drawn.

It is worth reflecting for a few moments on the preparation of missionaries for the sacrificial service that can be as tough and rough as this, if not more - even to the point of death. In his same 1951 conference address to the missionaries going out into remote field situations, Hudson told of a post war terror as the gospel began to blaze in Sarawak. Kelabits who had heard the gospel suddenly came down from their plateau, attacking and murdering their "fellow Christians" the Muruts on the Luping River. He writes that: "Everyone was in consternation. The old spectre of head hunting and tribal warfare seemed to rise again." Hudson and the fledgling post war church were in great danger of being destroyed in the cross fire of this ugly incident but he agreed to accompany the young inexperienced District Officer on the six day trek into the killing zone to investigate. Knowing the language, Hudson was able to counsel the tribes to Jesus peace and then he used his scientific skills to investigate carefully to show in the end that the trigger starting the blood feud was the "work of a Kelabit madman who had suddenly been overwhelmed by a homicidal mania." There was still fear but God helped both tribes to work through towards a victorious reconciliation. Such are the desperate miracles needed in early contact situations to defeat Satan. Calm, obedient biblical faith, prayer, training and experience are the key factors. Linguistic ability is also a great help! Civil authorities such as the inexperienced young District Officer sent out in this instance to investigate, are often amazed by miracles such as this, that come when faithful Christians trust and obey their Lord. Christians should not be surprised when this happens but the joy of such victory understandably gives way to amazed praise for the Lord's care. Such deliverance is at the very heart of gospel blaze.

If there is faithful obedience to God's calling then perceptions, vision and gifts are honed by the Holy Spirit to suit situations. It is amazing how the Lord arranges for faithful servants to be trained with the right skills, experience and fitness and be planted in the right place at just the right time. Jesus is the master strategist. Sabin speaks highly of Kerangkas and Kentuni, for example, who were there to help at just the right time. He wrote to his family saying:

"Kerangkas and Kentuni were dedicated and greatly used Dusan evangelists, converted in the early days of gospel presentation and will be remembered for their ministry. We depended so much upon them."

(*A record of the Ward Family* Page 20 - unpublished)

What of the call of Sabin himself? It was a strong enough call for Kumin to also recognise and accept. By faith she travelled with him to Borneo on an extended honeymoon "blind" as it were, for she had never been to Australia or South East Asia and the war stories were not much of an enticing travel brochure! The Korean War against Communism was at maximum effort to the north of Borneo, where there were also insurgents who caused problems later. South East Asia was a most volatile and dangerous part of the world. How do we become sure of God's call such that we are prepared to do something like this mission work amidst anxieties that mock our modern well-being concepts and are way out of any comfort zone we might prize? How did the Lord call Sabin so clearly? Researching back we find that three key events emerge as the foundation for his call to these dangerous wilds of Borneo.

Firstly, Sabin's father arranged to send him to the Anglican Caulfield Grammar School for no apparent particular reason, but it turned out be a powerful influence for mission. The boys in this school were taught to support missionaries by prayer and giving. Some staff went out to the mission field and through the crusader union, active in the school, Sabin became a sincere Christian with a missionary focus. Sabin wrote that:

"In the early 1930s at Caulfield Grammar we had regular talks by Australian overseas missionaries when on their home leave. All classes throughout the school collected missionary money to support, in a small way, the needs of the various field operations… We knew of the work of the BEM."

Secondly, on graduating from Melbourne University in 1938, Sabin was amongst a group of leaders at a Crusader Camp at Mt Eliza in Victoria who met BEM founders Hudson and Winsome Southwell at home on leave from Borneo. Sabin writes: "Hudson addressed us as we sat round the camp fire that night, in a most impressive way, so that Borneo became a reality."

Thirdly, in the following year, there was a major drama. Sabin was helping at the 1939 boy's camp held at Toolangi in the forest north of Melbourne. The commandant was Frank Davidson, another co-founder of BEM, also on leave home from Sarawak, Borneo, with his wife Enid and son John. Sabin describes the trauma of what happened at the camp:

"Forest fires of enormous ferocity, wiped out much of the country-side, forestry officers lost their lives; our camp was engulfed and we had to run for our lives. Frank gave a forthright lead and brought us to safety. Later that day as we drove back to Melbourne by bus, having lost all our belongings, Frank prepared to leave us and stood and said:

"Remember today and believe that we have been saved to serve!'"

In May 1939 of that same year, as war clouds were looming, Sabin attended the Melbourne University Evangelical Union house party. Again

Sabin met Frank Davidson, who was there with his wife Enid as houseparents. Sabin says that: "in informal chats and particularly at a slide showing one evening, Borneo began to have a real existence in our thinking."

War broke out and the Southwells and just Frank returned to Borneo to be imprisoned by the Japanese in the Kuching concentration camp. The Southwells both survived as a result of quite miraculous events, but Frank died just before the end of the war, and he is buried in Kuching. With full hearts Ellen and I viewed his grave on our 2023 visit to Kuching. Kind hosts, Libat and Anne Langub, took the trouble to show it to us and share insights to the considerable respect which Asian Christians extend to this brave missionary martyr, who never again saw his wife and son. This must have had a huge influence on Sabin as Frank's powerful words "saved to serve" echoed around in his mind.

Unmistakable events had thus formed a chain of guidance to mission for Sabin. A powerful missionary focus in a Christian school was followed by an exhilarating missionary BEM pioneer talk and then the very next year another BEM missionary pioneer had saved his life from the Toolangi bushfires with some typical Bornean jungle ingenuity and perseverance. Soon after this the same pioneer extolled the desperate needs in Borneo before dying there under the Japanese, who brought such despair to his countrymen on the Sandakan death marches. All were clear pointers that saturated Sabin's psyche throughout the troubled war years such that he finally realised whilst doing his PHD studies in Radio Physics in London post war, that he had been 'saved to serve' – in Borneo.

Sabin brought scientific skills and Kumin brought her medical knowledge and medicines to the work so that they were the right missionaries with the vision, experience and gifts that mattered in the right place at an important time of first contact.

Such outreach at this stage of mission was very practical, requiring caring for diseased indigenous folk and also technical help to get radio, generators, recording equipment and outboards for boats up and running in a scenario where the missionaries were penniless and there was little money for capital works. Just to keep the fragile little fabric covered aircraft running took a huge percentage of the available resources but these little planes were invaluable. Often, support for Sabin and Kumin sagged and they did not know whether they could survive. However, both had been tested and toughened up in the great depression and during and after the war. They knew that fervent faith and prayer could move mountains and were ready for the Labuk. God's planning was and is perfect.

Hudson Southwell and other founders have pointed to the various stages and needs for missionary endeavour at different times. Different skill sets and experience are needed in the different stages. The big mistake that needs to be avoided is being distracted by superior attitudes ingrained by cultural conditioning. These, often racist, attitudes use the technological advances of the west as a cloak for a false gospel of paternalistic, civilized well-being. Energy is directed into a take it or leave it injection of the "advances" of western culture for comfort that fails the test questions of ''are we all one in striving side by side for the gospel of Christ Jesus" and are we prepared to humbly learn from another culture as well as contribute to it?

A crucial decision point is reached when it becomes time for the expatriates to leave "their mission" and accept joyfully that after all the work it has at last grown into "the local people's church." This process may develop even further as these same returning missionaries might find their own home cultures have backslidden in the mean time and are in need of missionary help, especially in prayer, from the new young church they have just left.

It seems to me that, as represented very well by the Bornean experience, there are six stages of any new mission for Jesus. They refresh themselves as new outreach ventures are sparked into gospel blaze. The six stages are:

CALL, CONTACT, CONSOLIDATION, COMMITMENT, CORRECTION AND CELEBRATION.

In Borneo the first three stages went very fast after the war. After definite calling these stages involved meeting with village headmen and striving to get a hearing and then a foothold in remote longhouses. Parabolic gospel presentation was supported with simple follow-up material and pastoral visits. This led to some consolidation which involved getting regular worship going and stabilising basic survival with rejection of animism and magic charms, as well as giving advice about agriculture, house building using small saw mills, hygiene and medical matters. Consolidation also meant trying to improve communications with faster river craft and locating an airstrip nearby, where missionaries could be promptly supported and flown out for conferences. Also, potential key indigenous leaders could be flown out/in for advanced training and encouragement such as was available in Sarawak at the Lawas HQ Bible School.

It takes massive work over many years for the next commitment stage four to get established. Biblical translation into the local languages needs to be completed, bible schools established more locally, and culturally relevant church governance put in place. At this point it is often appropriate for the expatriates to leave. After this, return visits in person or by "letter" (= zoom today) are a useful correction follow up to further encourage and advise and if need be 'keep the ship on track' with biblically courageous encouragements and rebukes in love that are supported by explanation and exhortation towards pure doctrine.

The apostle Paul was very good at this. In just ten short busy years the Christian church was established as part of what F F Bruce has called *The Spreading Flame*. It blazed as a result of three missionary journeys used by God's Spirit. Paul answered a very definite call, which he continually revisited and renewed, and contacted potential believers with just a small, carefully vetted team at first, who helped many small churches to quickly form. Then he consolidated their function with a larger team that set up clever communications using letters and the Roman transport system to access, teach, advise and encourage the fledgling churches that were opened in key areas.

In the commitment stage, whilst supporting himself as a tentmaker, the apostle Paul settled down for several years in strategic places like Ephesus, fertilizing the new churches with in depth theological training that would thoroughly root them in the truth. Then, as he left a church area, he was alert to "return" by letter when there was a need for correction. Sometimes encouragement and exhortation were needed to correct wilting faith in the face of persecution. At other times what was needed was a firm rebuke followed by careful teaching to correct error and malpractice. He did not hold back in his letter to all the churches in Galatia that were in great danger of sacrificing the gospel of God's amazing grace for a useless non - salvation by Jewish law. "You foolish Galatians. Who has bewitched you?" he says in chapter 3: 1. This comes after starting his letter with a passionate challenge:

> "I am astonished that you are so quickly deserting the one who called you to live in the grace of Christ and are turning to a different gospel— 7 which is really no gospel at all. Evidently some people are throwing you into confusion and are trying to pervert the gospel of Christ."

> Galatians 1:6-7.

Many think that only encouragement is needed today and they are not comfortable with this corrective rebuke aspect of a healthy mission. However, the pioneering outreach of the gospel blaze in Borneo reminds us that a terrific spiritual war is taking place and often what is at stake justifies some collateral damage to our so called "finer western sensibilities." It is interesting to pause for a moment and ask do we in the west find it outrageous to think that one day the new world churches might have to return "the favour" and correct us? This does and is happening. Either way the kingdom of God wins.

The sixth and final stage of mission is joyfully eternal – celebration! This starts here in this life as we remember the work of our missionaries in spreading the gospel and celebrate wonderful achievements of the Holy Spirit in bringing the scriptures to us, reforming our churches of bad doctrine and adding new brothers and sisters from new cultures. But beyond time, the angels will help us ring out the praise for all this to our dear Father in heaven in the next life as we will, in some mysterious way beyond our ken at present, get to fellowship with each other all again. What a multitude of inexpressibly, wonderful, fulfilled, cleansed and perfect heirs of the Kingdom of God we will be! Praise be to King Jesus, the Firstborn from death to Life. (See Revelation 7:9)

From the middle of 1953, Kumin, Sabin and Ludin enjoyed a happy time getting used to each other as a family in Ranau for close on a year and a half as the new church there began to slowly transition towards the vital fourth commitment stage. Frontier outreach down the Labuk was put on hold whilst final consolidation activities around Ranau prepared the way for later missionaries such as Wes and Doreen Battle, who had the bible translation and deacon training skills to really grow the church. Doreen is a midwife and saw many of the local children safely into the world. She helped Wes start up a regular newspaper in Dusun to give the people something to improve their reading in readiness for the coming of the translated scriptures. Wes spoke Dusun well and went on many training treks right down the Labuk, once that did open up. Much of the bible translation had been well started by the Gollans and slowly the biblical text was translated into the Dusun language. Between 200 and 300 thousand Dusuns lived in this part of Borneo, so the embryonic church had to learn to read and then learn to interpret the bible accurately and apply it to make many big life changes and take on new Christian commitments. These included: the brave rejection of animistic practice, support of pastors and regular attendance at worship in the little thatched roofed churches that were being built. There was much preaching, teaching and pastoring to do in this last part of the consolidation stage. Ludin at this time was described by Sabin as a "blonde haired, happy little boy and very amenable". He was much loved and carried about by the people. His first awkward steps symbolised the first steps of a whole born again people learning to walk with Jesus in their new life as Christians.

Kumin held a regular medical practice in Ranau with some quite demanding tropical ulcers, goitres and sicknesses to treat. Penicillin worked wonders. Sabin further organised the HF radio network with only one frequency at his disposal as that was all that could be afforded. He looked at converting cheap engines with clever long shaft propeller drives suited to rapids and shallow water to drive the native boats and assist the transportation up and down rivers. The new Johnson outboards that had just become available were excellent but far too expensive, however the mission had their eye on these for the future.

There was a good grass airstrip at Ranau so the mission aircraft came and went with vital support that greatly encouraged the church and raised the morale of the missionaries. Sabin and Kerangkas went on regular treks to outlying villages to encourage, train and advise. All the while though, Sabin had his mind on the lost peoples of the Labuk, who were weeks of very harsh travel away from gospel help.

Midway through 1954 the Wards were coming to the end of their first term as missionaries and so they planned to travel to Australia in the spring of 1955. On the way out Sabin decided that they should have a concerted attempt to contact villagers in the lower Labuk and share the gospel and even consolidate a mission base somewhere there. There were sad but fond farewells with the now well established Ranau church and then the family flew to Sandakan by the beginning of 1955. From then on things happened very rapidly as often they do when the Spirit moves in significant ways.

The logistics must have been forming in Sabin's mind for some time, for the whole first contact stage was planned like a military operation with scientific precision, in which the assistance of Kerangkas travelling downstream from Ranau was key. Much equipment and supplies had to go into a central Labuk area to support the big outreach of the next few vital months. In a letter to Alan Belcher written from Sandakan on the 28 January 1955 some details emerge of the success of previous reconnoitres and all the planning that was done for first contact:

"We had a safe arrival here. Flew through fairly thick weather but Robertson, the pilot, did a good job. We only once or twice saw the Labuk, as we were at 8000 feet but on one occasion we were able to recognise the location … the 10hp Johnsons arrived here on today's ship. One available to us but the Sandakan agent has had to get authority from Jesselton to give us a discount. This is not to hand. I left Kerangkas and Kentuni the task of getting 20 coolie loads of equipment overland to the Labuk by the 15th February. Have arranged to meet him then at Klagan Jamu."

Where Sabin managed to get a new Johnson outboard from is a mystery, but soon it was pushing him and a boatload of helpers and supplies up against the current to meet Kerangkas. Unfortunately all the adventures that followed are lost to history but with an enormous effort they did set up an entirely new mission base. Within a few months a small house was built in a supportive village at Nangoh, and Kumin and Ludin were moved there with one house girl from Sandakan to help. It was very rough and wild and Kumin was left by herself with no communications quite often as Sabin moved up and down river visiting villages and trying to push hard towards the consolidation stage. There was one other problem. Now Kumin was 6 months pregnant with baby number two. One wonders about the wisdom of her being away from Sandakan at this time, but it is in keeping with the outreach habit of the period to include the family as part of the evangelism, so that the people could see them all trusting God through their inevitable suffering. Kumin did not appear to have much choice in the matter and later she was to assert some quite strong medical viewpoints about this. The practice was to have some dire consequences later. However, Kumin managed to survive and get out with Sabin and Ludin just in time to take the ship to Brunei alone to have Christopher (Andreas) on the 3rd of August, whilst Sabin looked after Ludin in Sandakan.

The consolidation stage had been achieved, but only just and in much haste with some dire bumps, however, a mission station in the jungle was established ready for the next missionary couples coming out to replace the Wards. In an amazing letter from Alan Belcher to Sabin on the 16th August 1955, there is quite an air of normality of mission base operations being established with the new Labuk outpost:

"We rejoiced to hear the news of Christopher Andrew ... Madge says that Laura looks well. We have made all the necessary arrangements about the Nappers and Tagal and Yamu residing in the Labuk area... Tagal is very apprehensive ... until he knows something of the language ... this step for them is bigger than our leaving home and coming to Borneo. .. the almost complete lack of (organisational) precedent does not make it easier."

(Mission letters 1955)

The context of this comment is the hope that the Dusun villagers would support the new missionaries themselves, right from the beginning. The concern of the mission was in not wanting to start a precedent of outside support. There were many problems to work through and the consolidation stage looked like being very hard and rough with minimal support.

One bright spot was the aviation program that continued faithfully to spread a mantle of security and encouragement wherever it operated. It was undergirded by much prayer and there was never a major accident. In the same letter, Alan Belcher says:

"If you are able to give Bruce (the pilot – Bruce Morton) your suggestions about the possible airstrip at Nangoh, then he can look at it from the air and give you his suggestions and recommendations … we consider that if the location at Nangoh is settled then we should think about putting in a strip."

An airstrip was one of the hallmarks of having achieved the consolidation stage of mission and this did happen at Nangoh. Bruce Morton was able to extract missionaries for help and encouragement and fly in rice and supplies at times when there were dire starvation challenges. There are many stories about the wobbly transition towards the commitment stage but these must be for future research and another time. Bruce Morton's pilot's log would make fascinating reading as a starting point.

The new Ward family of four left Borneo for Australia on the 4th of September 1955. After much reflection, discussion and prayer, James and Laura decided not to return to Borneo for another term with BEM for a number of reasons. One was that James's scientific career looked most promising and he felt that he could make a significant contribution to society and for Jesus in this. Another was the needs of the children from whom the parents did not want to be parted. But perhaps the most telling of all was the realisation that their service had really been best suited to the first three stages of mission and that different skill sets and aptitudes were needed for the next two. They were still to support BEM and visit the mission field again with each of their eventual four children, but their ministries lay in other areas than BEM missionary service. With new arterial roads, associated commerce and political change, the days of the pioneer first contact missionary in the wild, remote Bornean interior were over.

Laura reflected back on the missionary days in Borneo and wrote:

"During my busy life in Ranau, Jim was often away on extensive evangelisation visits to the animistic villages in the headwaters of the mighty Kinabatangan River, or to the lower reaches of the Labuk River near the East coast of Borneo. As the only European woman amongst numerous Dusun families I was never lonely or felt unsafe. Jim had installed high frequency radio communications to link up the main BEM mission stations in Sarawak and Sabah. This was valuable to complement the Mission's aviation operations and to pass on medical advice or instructions to the hard pressed isolated missionary groups. I was able to transmit from Ranau radio messages spoken to Jim, which he received on his miniature, battery driven radio receiver – often when he was camped on a river bank with a makeshift aerial rigged to a nearby tree… At Ranau, a simple Bible School using the Malay language for teaching was introduced on the basis of two weeks of school / farming and then two weeks for evangelising. Regular open air gospel presentations … were conducted by Dusun Christian leaders in the village on market days."

(Unpublished Ward family history).

James also looked back in reflection and wrote:

"In these former BEM fields of endeavour the Lord has caused to be created an indigenous church known as SIB (In Malay: Sidang Injil Borneo). Now over 1000 village and city churches meet in this name. Remarkably the SIB itself is sending its own missionaries to work in animistic tribal communities in other South East Asian countries. Today there is a well ordered Bornean ministry that challenges all generations everywhere to heed the call of the Lord to witness to His redeeming work. We can praise our Lord for all this!"

(Unpublished Ward family history).

CHAPTER EIGHT

Three Stories from the Pioneering Days.

**A 1955 Labuk story about baby Ludin and
the gospel as remembered by Kumin.**

After ministry in the Ranau area, which saw the church grow and become
strong and Ludin thrive on the care of many as he took his first steps, it
was finally time in 1955 for a first furlough and the Wards decided to leave
Borneo and return to Australia. Later this became a permanent departure
as scientific work beckoned for Sabin, and Kumin was pregnant with a
brother for Ludin, to be called Chris (Andreas). Before he was born, however, it was decided to have a last outreach to the villages set in the wild
jungle along the mighty Labuk River.

The Ranau church gave the Wards a sad but fond farewell in late
1954 and soon an overloaded Dragon Rapide, twin engine biplane, stag-
gered into the air off the Ranau strip with the Wards and their gear and
headed for Sandakan. At the controls was Ex Second World War fighter

pilot Robbie Robinson, who was to marry a BEM missionary called Margaret.

In just a few minutes The Dragon flew quickly over the Labuk and the route of the horrific war time death marches that had lasted for several years in the thick jungle at a time of deep despair. Now a gospel light had been kindled amongst those below and it was to blaze more and more across Sabah. But along the primitive Labuk there was still much darkness.

Soon the Wards had stored their gear at Sandakan and moved up into the lower reaches of the Labuk, where sympathetic tribesmen built them a very small one bedroom hut. Eiyong, a house girl from Sandakan, came to help. The headman in this village was very supportive of those bringing the gospel but the headman of the village across on the other side of the river was not and asked them to leave as he believed their witchdoctor had all the truth and gave all the help that was needed.

Sabin left Kumin and travelled up and down the river preaching the gospel to whoever would hear. He was driving very hard to move up a stage from first contact to a consolidated mission station status. He knew that he only had another few months before leave back to Australia when other missionaries would be coming to replace them, so he was focused on using every moment for gospel outreach and left Kumin to fend for herself. It is hard to know for sure but there are indications that he was also thinking that this leave might extend to a permanent departure from the mission, as he pursued scientific work, so he wanted to leave the best legacy he could.

Kumin, now alone with just Ludin and the house girl was heavily pregnant and there were no communications or viable back up evacuation services. She was shocked one terrible night to find that Ludin had developed a bad fever and was delirious and seemed to be deteriorating very quickly. Kumin was a medical doctor, though, who had helped many in Ranau, and knew a little about tropical medicine. She did what she could and resorted to much prayer. In the morning there were spots and the temperature settled and she realised that Ludin had measles with a very bad fever, which the medicines seemed to have controlled. She remembered there had been cases of this in the village across the river.

Kumin, immediately returned to this resistant village across the river and told them that her son had measles and did they need help? Sadly, the headman said quietly that "yes, we had two children die last night from this measles fever."

"Why didn't you come to me?" said Kumin. Then the headman said diffidently that he didn't want to get caught up in European's preaching the gospel, as it was up to the "witchdoctors to heal and look after the sick."

"That was the worst possible thing to do" said Kumin. "My Lord Jesus has given us medicines and He saved my little boy."

Soon afterwards many in the whole area became Christian as the BEM Nangoh outpost and airstrip were set up.

The Lord gives and takes away but always furthers His purposes. The missionary couple relieving the Wards also went up into the Labuk outpost but there they lost their first baby. They stayed firm in faith, however, and continued to witness for Jesus.

Such is the cost of discipleship. Always though, the people were watching the love and generous commitment of these pioneer gospel bearers and they empathised with their sufferings. They realised that they were committed to sharing a precious faith in the Lord Jesus who could make them all caring brothers and sisters in one body of followers of the firstborn – this same Jesus who had died for them as well.

Many had also witnessed the strong loving faith of the missionaries interned by the Japanese in the Second World War and then being prepared to return after the death marches that saw the demise of so many of their countrymen. Now they knew that such commitment went as far as boldly facing death, which, gloriously, was seen to have lost its sting. Satan was defeated.

Strong seeds were sown on fertile ground.

Now gospel light blazes in Borneo!

A 1962 story about Sabin standing firm, as witnessed by a nine year old Ludin.

After leaving Borneo, Sabin and Kumin settled into activities of science, medicine, rearing a family of now three boys - as Alistair (Rudi) had arrived - and doing church work, which involved speaking about Borneo, so that more would pray and support the mission work there. After seven years away, they were in a position to revisit Ranau. For the Christmas of 1961 the three boys and their parents stayed in a new wooden house opposite the church inhabited by the Battle family, who were then away on leave.

One night there was a loud commotion at the door. There was no electricity and the wood stove and kerosene lamps cast eerie shadows up the walls and across the ceilings. I pushed my way out of the mosquito netting to see what was happening. It was like having a nightmare at first. Although I was an onlooker I thought that I might quickly get sucked into the trauma of anguished cries and ghostly, dancing shadows competing to extinguish the calm but urgent tones of my father, Sabin.

A very distressed villager was trembling in front of my father, clutching a strange cloth package as his friend beside him tried to explain. Both were very afraid and I could feel the extreme apprehension and a massive sense of threat invading the room.

The friend explained that the young man had decided to follow Jesus and give his life to God but he was terrified about getting rid of the witchdoctor's lucky cloth charm that had "protected" him all his life from the evil spirits who were now very angry. He had never unwrapped the charm but it had been his forever and he had been brought up to trust it and keep it safe. He had tried unsuccessfully many times to bring himself to destroy the charm. Now he cried out for help from my father to stand firm against the evil we could all feel, and to help him by destroying it, for he could not.

My father saw me standing wide eyed and beckoned me over to the table where he had placed the charm. I cannot remember his exact words but the effect of them was that Jesus is stronger than any evil spirits and we need to look for His victory now. I think I trusted Dad more than Jesus at that point, as I yet had to make a full decision to follow Jesus myself, but I stood still whilst Dad serenely untied the cords around the cloth charm.

A candle with needles sticking into it was revealed, together with a few beads. It was anti-climactic but I was amazed by the intense anxiety etched on the young charm keeper's face. My father's placid confidence did calm him, though.

Dad showed us close up the beads, needles and the candle lying on the dirty, rotting cloth, so that we could see that they were all just very ordinary things. Then with a single, confident gesture he opened the grill gate to the wood stove and threw them in where the old cloth caught quickly and blazed brightly. After a sharp cry from the young villager, all was quiet and a warm comforting glow seem to settle throughout the room.

Whenever I want to define the fruit of joy in the work of the Spirit I just have to remember this young man's face after his charm was destroyed and his Satan burden was lifted. Shining, delighted eyes and a huge smile of jubilation suffused everything. He was profuse in his thanks and relief. He was safe! Nothing bad had happened! Here was very personal proof of the supreme reality of Jesus the very son of the living God conquering all evil.

Dad could be stern at times, but, in a way I could not remember seeing before, now he was smiling expansively with illuminated delight, as he cheerfully farewelled two young men into the dark night, only now it was alight with their renewed peace and hope in the Lord.

A typical story of ministry at Ranau and along the Labuk River of the sixties, as told by BEM missionary Bulan Battle. The Labuk was now rapidly approaching the commitment stage of mission stability.

The Way of the Spirit is so different to the way of the world ...

Almost every two months my husband Dawat with some deacons from Ranau church went to a village for four weeks to run a short term Bible school for Dusuns who had "followed Christianity" (Ikut sahaja). On hearing the pure gospel they were born again. Dawat had the advantage of speaking Dusun. These schools created very alive and active churches. A number of times Dawat and his team walked three days to Labuk villages and I remember one trip in particular.

After Dawat left home for the Labuk in 1964, I developed amoebic dysentery, confirmed by a doctor in Sandakan. The pain and dysentery left me feeling weaker and weaker. Joy was about five years old and I mentioned to her that it might be good if I could contact Lawas Mission Head Quarters and ask the pilot to drop a letter to Dawat asking him to come home. However, I did not have peace about doing that.

Next morning, I was sitting on the floor with my head on the bed, too weak to pray but decided to repeat **Psalm 103**. I reached verse 3 and as I said "who heals all your diseases," **John 17:17** came to my mind. I told that thought to go away so I could continue with the psalm, but it came back three times. Then I realised I needed to heed it. "What does John 17:17 say, I asked myself." Jesus was praying to His Father just before Gethsemane and said, "Your Word is truth." I put that verse and Psalm 103:3, "who heals all your diseases" together and said, "Father in Jesus Name I declare that Your Word is truth and by the stripes of Jesus I am healed."

Within twenty minutes the terrible aches stopped, and I no longer needed to run to the toilet.

When Dawat returned home, I told him about my healing and he said that one day the chief of the village who was then not a Christian, came to him and said, "We don't want you in this village. We don't want this Christian teaching. Go home! You will have a letter dropped from the sky telling you to go home!"

Dawat did not heed what was said because he knew it was not from God. The quite large group of believers were enjoying all the teaching. What would have happened to those believers if I had gone ahead and asked for that letter to be dropped?

EPILOGUE

From a Spark to a Flame

Now the SIB / BEM church is distinguishing itself with respectful cele-bration, as its members thank God for His rich provision in sending the missionaries at just the right time. They are acquitting themselves well in applying the Word of God so as to be presented mature in Christ. They now stand firm for Him as they hold the pearl without price, the treasure of the Kingdom of God. They look forward eagerly to fellowship with other sisters and brothers all over the world. Persecution will always return but faith and rich, deep, prayer abound all the more, so that God's grace is eas-ily sufficient to sustain the blaze for His glory!

John 17: 13 – 17 is a most apt way to pause our exploration of all that is happening in the blaze of Gospel Light that is flashing out in Borneo. No doubt there will be many future chapters of gospel adventure that will be written, especially as revival comes to the cities. Many are continuing in the old missionary traditions of counting the cost of being a disciple of Jesus, protected from the evil one. Whilst living for Him wherever they are called, they are not of this world anymore, but of the Kingdom of God.

Everyone is invited to join this Kingdom. Entry is not earned by doing good things or making sacrifices. It is gifted by the Lord Almighty on the basis of our humble belief and trust in Jesus.

In this most precious passage, Jesus lets us hear Him speaking to His Father about this:

[13] "I am coming to you now, but I say these things while I am still in the world, so that they may have the full measure of my joy within them. [14] I have given them your word and the world has hated them, for they are not of the world any more than I am of the world. [15] My prayer is not that you take them out of the world but that you protect them from the evil one. [16] They are not of the world, even as I am not of it. [17] Sanctify them by the truth; your word is truth. [18] As you sent me into the world, I have sent them into the world. [19] For them I sanctify myself, that they too may be truly sanctified."

And so the honey sweet acclamation of Psalm 103 is truly manifest.

This sustained Bulan at a time of dire need.

It can sustain you and me as well:

Psalm 103: 1–5 of David:

¹ Praise the LORD, my soul;
all my inmost being, praise his holy name.
² Praise the LORD, my soul,
and forget not all his benefits—
³ who forgives all your sins
and heals all your diseases,
⁴ who redeems your life from the pit
and crowns you with love and compassion,
⁵ who satisfies your desires with good things
so that your youth is renewed like the eagle's.

What should our response be to both the cost and the wonder of Gospel Blaze?

The chorus of Graham Kendrick's great song *God of the Poor - beauty for Brokenness* guides us in a most appropriate prayer to our dear Lord to kindle this blaze:

God of the poor, Friend of the weak,
Give us compassion, we pray.
Melt our cold hearts; let tears fall like rain;
Come, change our love from a spark to a flame.

• Sabah is the northern State of Borneo, now East Malaysia. The state of Sarawak with capital Kuching is to the south. The BEM headquarters was in the middle at Lawas. In 2023 we flew into Kuching from Kuala Lumpur, then up to Kota Kinabalu and drove to Ranau and Sandakan. We flew back via Singapore, which was the approach/departure base for most of the early BEM missionaries. *(Google Maps 2024)*

• BEM pioneer founder - Hudson Southwell with wife Winsome and son Lukut. In 1932 Hudson heard from Botanists, Mr and Mrs Clements, that the Dusun or Kadazan people in Sabah needed visiting. He explored the Ranau area in 1936 and discovered that "the people knew little or nothing about God but they were quite open and willing to talk about Him." BEM made it a focus.

• Ranau Airport in the 1950s. BEM Auster Auto car left and Dragon Rapide right. Later Prestwick Pioneers were also used servicing some very challenging airstrips.

• Sabin in 1952.

• The 1939 Houseparty group from Melbourne University Evangelical Union where Sabin felt called to mission work in Borneo. Sabin is in the back row *(3rd from left)*. House parents were BEM co-founder Frank Davidson *(back row 5th from the right)* and his wife Enid *(middle row 4th from the right)*. Frank died in Kuching under Japanese occupation in 1945. Win Burrows *(far right of middle row)* became a mission nurse who served with distinction for many years in Sarawak.

Kumin in 1952.

• Ranau church in 1954, now into the commitment stage of mission. Here they farewell Sabin, Kumin and Ludin.

Dusun ladies helped Kumin with the home duties and health services. Kumin allowed Ludin to be "adopted" a bit by the Dusuns but she kept a very close eye on him and gave him the very best medical care and much affection.

· Ludin was much cared for by the Dusuns. They took him everywhere around their church activities. While he learned to walk and be self-sufficient they learned to walk with Jesus, so he was an important symbol of hope and growth in the gospel, despite all the inevitable mistakes and setbacks.

· The mission aircraft and river transport were used to ferry missionaries and their families into the Lawas HQ in Sarawak for occasional conferences - for training, strategy organisation and encouraging fellowship.

· As Christianity spread throughout Borneo, simple wood churches were built and became havens for joyous worship free of fears of evil spirits and witch doctor magic. Soon there was a need for suitably qualified indigenous pastors, so Bible Schools had to be established.

In the days of the head hunters and village feuds, there had to be great vigilance against attack and the headman's authority and caution continued as the missionaries asked for access to longhouses. They had to demonstrate they came with a message of Jesus' love and not a motive of exploitation.

A new mission aircraft – an Auster Autocar - is dedicated to pioneering work in primitive conditions. BEM Field Chairman Alan Belcher (left) stands beside veteran ex war-time pilot Bruce Morton, as fervent prayers are said for safe operations. These were answered as there was never a serious accident.

Light aircraft and radio made an enormous difference to missionaries isolated and often alone in extremely remote and rugged locations. Sabin established a one frequency HF radio network that linked Sabah outposts back to mission headquarters at Lawas in Sarawak. He could make contact from a portable battery transmitter with an aerial strung up at river camp sites. Kumin was reassured by such frequent contact, whilst he was away.

The joy of the genuine 4 seat Auster Autocar. It greatly improved aviation versatility. Here pilot Bruce Morton and his wife Ruth are in the front of the new Auster and BEM field chairman Alan Belcher and his wife Madge are in the back.

• Short, rough bush strips like this, often beside turbulent river bends that spat unexpected wind gusts out on approach, tested all the skills of the dedicated pilots, especially in bad weather.

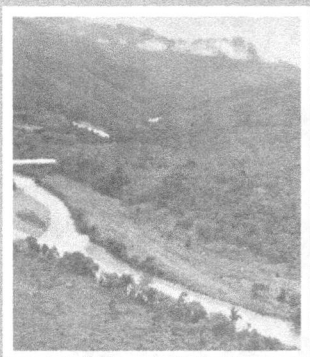

• As the airstrips were often marginal, every metre counted, so this STOL twin Prestwick Pioneer is hauled with its tail back into the bushes to give it the best chance of a successful take off.

• Mission aircraft tamed the jungle. Messages were dropped when there were no landing sites in very rugged areas. Aerial capability had a huge impact on the people and has been wonderfully exploited throughout the world by the Missionary Aviation Fellowship (MAF), which was encouraged in Australia by BEM pilots Bruce Morton and Ken Cooper.

• Dawat and Bulan Battle and their family were flown in/out of Ranau in the 1960s. They were practical, tough trekking, gifted linguists who stayed into the 1970s helping, with others, to advance the commitment stage of mission so wonderfully. The Holy Spirit used them greatly to feed the gospel blaze.

• Here mission pilot Ken Cooper's wife Joan, visits Dawat Battle in Ranau as they encourage helpers at one of the many schools for Deacon training. The new native pastors were very young Christians in much need of culturally sensitive, biblically precise training. The Battles did much to fulfil this need amongst the Dusuns.

• Three early post-war mission pioneers: Horrie Hamer, Sam Gollan (Ranau bible translator before the Wards arrived) and Ken Cooper, one of the mission pilots. Taken in Sydney in 1948 as they prepared to leave for Borneo.

• Mt Kinabalu, 13,435ft, snapped below by Sabin on one of the many flights into Ranau in the early 1950s, before passable roads made access much easier. At this altitude it is no wonder that Kumin sometimes complained of feeling a bit dizzy.

- Australian BEM Prayer Warriors supporting Sabin and Kumin meet in Swanwick, UK, in 1948.
Back Row: Dorothy Mowll, Archbishop Donald Robinson, Archbishop and Anglican Primate of Australia, Howard Mowll.
Front Row: Canon Stan Kurrle, Dr James Ward (Sabin), Thomas Hammond, Principal of Moore Theological College.

- John Stott was a great supporter of BEM and visited Sabin and Kumin in Townsville. He officiated at their 1951 wedding as Kumin attended All Souls church in London. John Stott organised a prayer group which prayed and sent funds out to BEM. *(Picture taken by Lantana)*

- Kumin with a BEM evangelistic team at Peginatan about to divide into two groups for the Labuk River descent through some rough jungle and river rapids.
From left: Mjow, Keradi, Kendeer, Kumin, Iki, Udan with baby Paraq.

- Udan and Iki with baby Paraq. Very early native missionaries to the Dusans in the Ranau area. They arrived before Sabin and Kumin and did important foundational consolidation work. They were a great encouragement to Sabin and Kumin.

• Trevor White (Asang – left) and Kerangkas shepherded the young churches around Ranau. Trevor was a carpenter who taught the young Christians how to make more substantial homes cheaply, using sawn planks from his saw mill.
Kerangkas was ideally suited to facilitating the early stages of mission whilst Asang married a Bornean girl and stayed in the area. He was a gifted linguist and church builder.

• Matalung and Kerangkas.

• The native Christian boatmen built for pregnant Kumin this lovely sun shelter hut on the river boat used to explore the Labuk.

• Sabin worked with the boatmen to install a tiny engine that greatly improved performance especially up current.

• Typical river boating Borneo style. The bow hands and steersmen needed crucial skills to work in split second harmony to negotiate the fierce rapids.

• With very little money and no access to outboard motors the engine installation with impeller for shallow water operations was a typical piece of Ward engineering and Aussie ingenuity. Sabin's father, Walter, was an amateur fishing boat builder and all the skills were there when needed.

• Shooting the rapids – this is a very gentle patch but still best viewed from the river bank!

The tiny one bedroom house built in the remote Labuk for the Wards in 1955. Early houses built for the missionaries initially were typical of all native dwellings in the early days – simple bamboo floored, thatched rooved huts on stilts. Very flimsy but easily replaced. They were in constant need of maintenance.

- First baptismal service outside the little Ward House beside the Labuk River. Now the BEM had consolidated outreach in one of the remotest areas with a proper church, visited here by Matalung and Kentuni.

- A saw mill provided cheap planks for more substantial buildings for the early Christians who were very poor and had to transition away from subsistence living. Asang used his saw mill extensively and whole new villages such as Bongkud were set up. This helped consolidate the first contact work of mission operations.

• One the more substantial plank houses that Asang taught the people at Bongkud to build.

• The "new" mission wood house built in Ranau in 1960 was well founded and properly finished with a good steel roof. It has lasted well and been extended and is still used today by a pastor of the Ranau church.

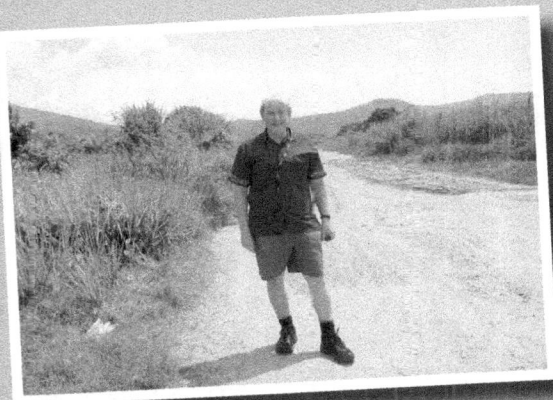

* Here, in 1954, Ludin takes his first steps on the Ranau airstrip, which was the only really flat play area around on which to learn to walk. The photo was taken by a visiting Christian from America who could afford to buy colour film which was very rare in those days. Financial support was below minimal – everyone was so poor. But the First Steps symbol to the people was clear.

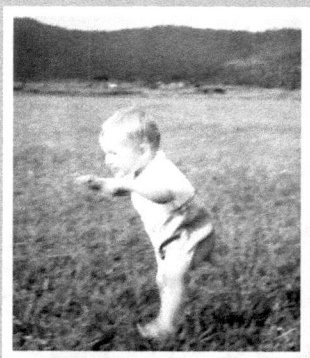

* Here in 2023, Ludin walks on the now disused and overgrown Ranau airstrip of his babyhood. So much has happened in the last 70 years. The gospel blaze is a wonderful highlight!

* In 1955 Sabin and Kumin return with Ludin and Andreas to Melbourne and the home near Elwood beach of Sabin's parents. Four years of rich missionary service completed and the Bornean church is beginning to blaze.

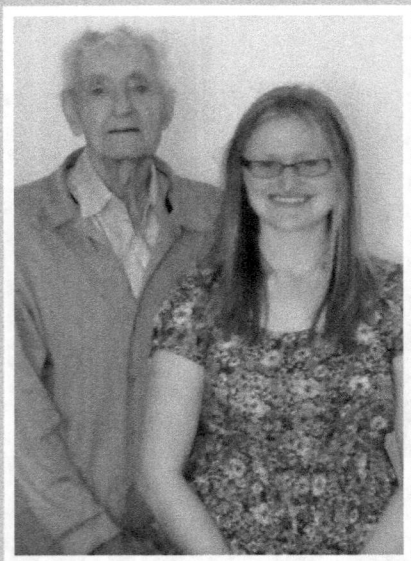

• Sabin's granddaughter, Christie, served us at the 2012 Mission Pioneers reunion; now, after practising as a teacher for some years, she is at Sydney Missionary Bible College doing a masters in theology as she contemplates mission work and listens for a call. The blaze continues through the generations!

• 2012 Mission pioneers reunion in Sydney. Dawat with Bulan seated in front, Ken Coleman with his wife Maureen seated, Ray Cunningham standing behind Kumin seated and Sabin and Ludin standing together behind Evelyn Cunningham seated.

• Missionary Trevor White (Asang) visits the Wards in their Townsville home in the 1970s. *From left*: Hilary (Lantana), Chris (Andreas), Trevor, Kumin, Sabin, Ludin between two of Trevor's daughters Delia *(left)* and Rosmie *(right)* as well as Madge, Kumin's faithful prayer warrior mother.
Picture taken by third Ward son, Alistair (Rudi).

• Sabin and Dawat share many tales of Contact, Consolidation and Commitment to spiritual growth in mission. Together they represent the work in Ranau from the 1950s to the 1970s, BEM to SIB.

* Missionaries came out to the coast for holidays especially at Labuan where there was accommodation for them. Here Ellen and Jim (Ludin), son of Sabin, enjoy typical tropical refreshment on the Sarawak beaches of the South China Sea.

* Sarawak River, Kuching – 2023 arrival back in Borneo.

* Ellen and Jim with kind Kuching Christians, Libat and Anne Langub. They have both grown up in subsistence villages and accessed good education through the missionaries and now, in professional practice, they serve the church with their legal skills.

* The large BEM /SIB church in Kuching.

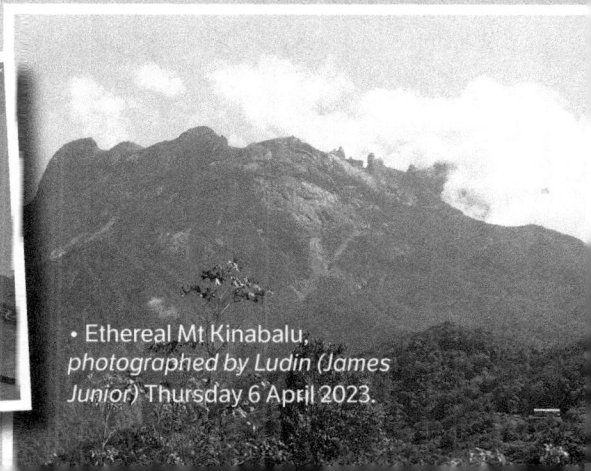

* Ethereal Mt Kinabalu, *photographed by Ludin (James Junior)* Thursday 6 April 2023.

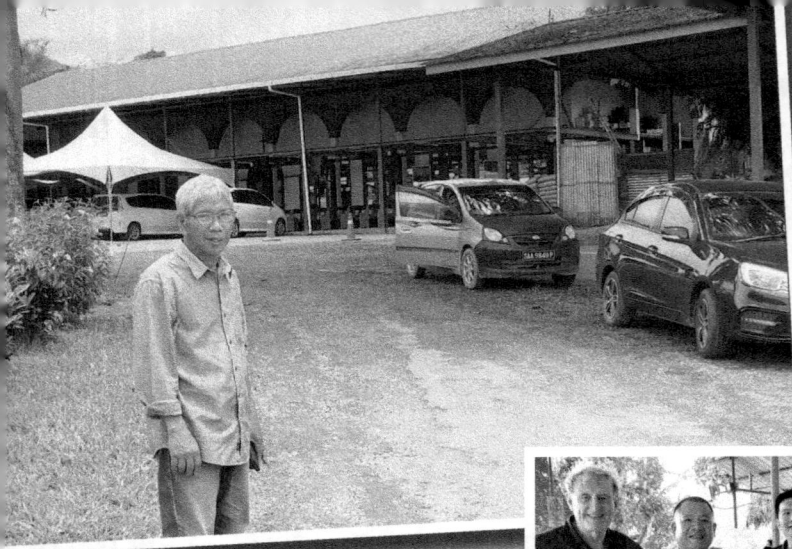

• Paul Kerangkas stands in front of the thriving Ranau church in 2023, indicative of many Bornean SIB / BEM self-supporting churches alight with the gospel today in Borneo. Adjoining the church building to the right of the picture is the memorial to the death march massacres.

• Christian leaders from Kota Kinabalu take us out for breakfast - 2023

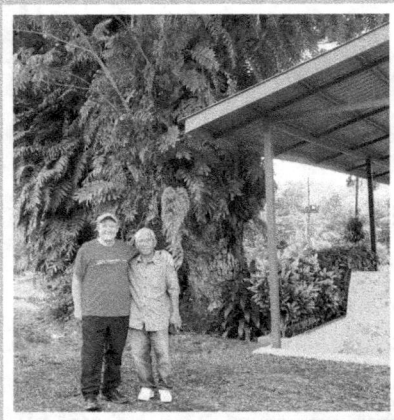

• *[over page]* The congregation at Bongkud have outgrown their church so they are now building a much bigger one themselves –out of steel! Asang would have been most impressed.

• Ludin and Paul Kerankas in front of Sabin's raintrees beside the Ranau church (to the left). The growth of these remarkable trees symbolises the growth of the gospel work in Ranau. To the right is the memorial museum to the sacrifices of the Sandakan Death marches.

Ranau church leaders invite us to breakfast fellowship – Easter Sunday 2023.

The visiting pastor to the Ranau church preaching passionately, fluently, biblically and without notes on Easter Sunday, 2023.

Paul Kerangkas interprets for Ludin turning English into Malay, just as Paul's father used to translate for Sabin turning Malay into Dusun, back in the 1950s.

• The tropical sunsets of Borneo are truly magnificent and for us they symbolise the glory to be given to God for the exquisite movement of His Spirit that has fanned the flames of Christian faith in Borneo, into a heart-warming blaze.

• Paul's son Luther, Paul's sister Muriam, who looked after Ludin as a baby, Paul's brother Maibul and Paul's wife Dorothy enjoy yet another breakfast fellowship with Paul and Ludin sharing photos and swapping many stories. A magical time!

• Sabin and Kumin enjoyed many happy and fruitful years in Townsville and their big home near the sea was visited by BEM folk from Borneo. Such tales were told! The whole Bornean odyssey was used many times to encourage Aussies walking their first steps with Jesus.

• The four Ward children – Ludin, Andreas, Lantana and Rudi - in 2019 at the graves of Sabin and Kumin in St Kilda Cemetery, near the Melbourne Bible Institute site, where the BEM was born, by the grace of God, in 1928. They glorify God for His faithfulness throughout all the years of the commitment of many to the Gospel Blaze in Borneo.

www.ingramcontent.com/pod-product-compliance
Lightning Source LLC
LaVergne TN
LVHW021613080426
835510LV00019B/2551